# THE THIRTEENTH CHAIR

*A Play in Three Acts*

BY
BAYARD VEILLER

## SAMUEL FRENCH

NEW YORK, N. Y.          HOLLYWOOD, CALIF.
25 WEST 45th STREET      7623 SUNSET BLVD.
SAMUEL FRENCH, Ltd., LONDON
SAMUEL FRENCH (Canada), Ltd., TORONTO

# MR. AND MRS. NORTH

Mystery-comedy. 3 acts. By Owen Davis, based on the stories by Frances and Richard Lockridge. 16 males, 4 females. Interior. Modern costumes.

Amateurs may now enjoy the comedy which delighted New York and summer theatre audiences for months. Pam and Gerald North are a pleasant young married couple living in Greenwich Village in New York. Upon their return to the apartment after a brief absence, Gerald opens his closet door—and out falls the dead body of a strange man. The police are called and the investigation starts. All their friends are suspected and even Pam and Gerald have difficulty in explaining certain things to the inspector. Gerald is worried, but Pam is pleased to be thought so naughty. It is Pam who finally unmasks the murderer with her ingenious accusations, and of course, the explanations follow in quick order. "I like it. These are real folk caught in a web of plausible and amusing situations. There is laughter in it and a touch of sentiment, a craftily sustained suspense."— *N. Y. Daily News.*

(Royalty, $35.00.) Price, 85 cents.

# THE PHILADELPHIA STORY

Comedy. 3 acts. By Philip Barry. 9 males, 6 females. Interior. Modern costumes.

The smash hit of Broadway and Hollywood with Katharine Hepburn in the leading role. Tracy Lord is a cold beauty who has divorced C. K. Dexter Haven of her own set and is about to be married to Kittredge, a successful young snob. Unpleasant circumstances, hinging on her father's dissatisfaction with the lack of understanding and warmth in her character, force Tracy to allow her very fashionable wedding to be photographed and reported by a worldly-wise camera-woman and a class-conscious young reporter who is really a fine writer. After the pre-wedding party, Tracy and the reporter share a swift and illuminating look at themselves and take a moonlight dip in the pool. Tracy, somewhat thawed and thinking with vivid clarity, calls off the wedding to Kittredge, and after refusing the reporter's proposal, decides to remarry Dexter Haven, promising in future to be a human being. "The dialogue is smart . . . rapid, sparkling, and rich in wit." —*New York World-Telegram.*

(Royalty, $50.00.) Price, 85 cents.

# THE THIRTEENTH CHAIR

## A PLAY IN THREE ACTS

BY
### BAYARD VEILLER

NEW YORK
SAMUEL FRENCH
PUBLISHER
25 WEST 45TH STREET

LONDON
SAMUEL FRENCH, LTD.
26 SOUTHAMPTON STREET
STRAND

## *"The Thirteenth Chair"*
### *All Rights Reserved*

"The Thirteenth Chair" was produced by William Harris, Jr., at the 48th Street Theatre, New York, on November 20, 1916, with the following cast:

HELEN O'NEILL.............*Katherine La Salle*
WILL CROSBY....................*Calvin Thomas*
MRS. CROSBY.....................*Martha Mayo*
ROSCOE CROSBY..................*Gardner Crane*
EDWARD WALES...................*S. K. Walker*
MARY EASTWOOD..................*Eva Condon*
HELEN TRENT.................*Sarah Whitford*
GRACE STANDISH....................*Rose Aiken*
BRADDISH TRENT...................*Charles Lait*
HOWARD STANDISH................*Walter Lewis*
PHILIP MASON..................*George Graham*
ELIZABETH ERSKINE...........*Alice Claire Elliott*
POLLOCK..........................*A. J. Hendon*
ROSALIE LA GRANGE..........*Margaret Wycherly*
TIM DONAHUE.................*Harrison Hunter*
SERGEANT DUNN.................*Walter Young*
DOOLAN ..........................*Wm. Scott*

## THE CAST

HELEN O'NEILL.
WILL CROSBY.
MRS. CROSBY.
ROSCOE CROSBY.
EDWARD WALES.
MARY EASTWOOD.
HELEN TRENT.
BRADDISH TRENT.
HOWARD STANDISH.
PHILIP MASON.
ELIZABETH ERSKINE.
GRACE STANDISH.
POLLOCK.
MADAME ROSALIE LA GRANGE.
TIM DONOHUE.
SERGEANT DUNN.
DOOLAN.

## ACT I

The Italian Room in Roscoe Crosby's House.
TIME: Evening.

## ACT II

Same scene. Ten minutes later.

## ACT III

Same scene. A half an hour later.

# THE THIRTEENTH CHAIR

## ACT I

SCENE: *Italian Room in* ROSCOE CROSBY'S *Home.
A handsomely furnished square room, door
opening on stage down* L. *Door opening on
stage at back* L.C. *Large fireplace* C. *at back.
Door opening on stage* R.C.

*NOTE: Fireplace—antique firedogs—must
be large enough for men to make entrance coming down through chimney. Large window over*
R. *in arch. Platform one step high running full
length of window, which is three sashes long.
Trick blind on* C. *pane. Curtains on pole on*
C. *windows to work on cue. Up* C. *in front of
fireplace facing up stage, large Chesterfield sofa
two feet wide. Facing audience another large
Chesterfield sofa,* C., *sofas setting back to back.
At each end of sofas small console table. Console table at* R. *end of sofa is the trick table
which* ROSALIE *lifts.* R. *of the door,* R.C., *large
antique Italian chest.* L. *of door,* L.C., *large an-*

5

*tique chest. Vases on chests. On flat over* L., *large tapestry. Against wall over* L., *running up and down stage, long ornate Italian chest. At either end of this chest Italian lamps, seven feet high, standing on floor. On console tables at either end of sofa, table lamps. On console table* L. *end of sofa, fancy cigarettes, box with cigarettes and matchbox and ash tray, and below door down* L., *on flat, an antique clock. Below door down* L., *armchair.* L. *side of fireplace chair with cushion seat. On mantel two large antique vases.* R. *side of fireplace with cushion seat.* L. *side, below console table, large armchair. Over* R. *is a large library table sitting diagonally up and down stage. On table: book rack with four books, desk pad, stationery holder with stationery, pens, pencils, ink box, magazines, armchair back of table, chair below table, chair above table. On platform in window arch, long seat. Below window arch large armchair. Large wall lanterns, on up stage, and down stage, end of window arch. Plush Valence or drapery for windows. Rugs on ground cloth. On flat* R. *of doors up* R.C. *small-sized, painted image of the Virgin. Interior backing for door down* L., *up* L.C. *and* R.C. *Fireplace backing. Exterior backing for window over* R. *Off stage down* L., *run on floor, large Italian table with two bronze vases, and a shrine of the Virgin on it. Off stage* R.C. *are eight small chairs, to be brought on stage on cue during first act. In ceiling, directly over table* R., *is a double slot to hold knives. During first act, after* WILL *puts out table lamp, after* MISS EASTWOOD'S *scream, the knife, in down stage slot, is let down in sight of audience. Seen with point sticking in ceiling. Between second and third acts, the knife that falls on cue, during third act, is placed up stage slot in ceiling, with point downwards. Setting the knife down in view of audience in first act, as well as releasing the second knife so that it falls, and sticks in table during third act, is worked by strings off stage R.*

*(As the curtain rises MISS HELEN O'NEILL and WILLIAM CROSBY are discovered standing R.C. They are in each other's arms, and the rising curtain discloses them as they kiss. Window-shade down.)*

HELEN. I love you so.

WILLIAM. You are the most wonderful thing in all the world. *(She gives a little laugh and moves away from him a step R.)*

HELEN. I can't believe it.

WILL. That I love you?

HELEN. Oh, no, I'm sure of that.

WILL. If there's any doubt in your mind, I'll prove it again.

HELEN. They'll see us. *(He takes her in his arms again and kisses her. She laughs happily. And then, turning a little, stands with her cheek pressed against his)* Oh, my dear, my dear.

*(MRS. CROSBY, a fashionably dressed and extremely attractive woman, enters from door down left, closes door. She stops for a moment, and watches the lovers and then with a little laugh comes toward them. MRS. CROSBY is fifty-five and looks ten years younger, she has charm, beauty and kindliness, and is as far removed*

*from the typical stage mother, as it is possible for the management to picture.)*

MRS. CROSBY. *(Coming to* C. *a step—*WILL *breaks a step)* Don't move, you look so comfortable! *(They start apart)* Well, are you happy? *(To* R.C. WILL *pats* MRS. CROSBY *on arm.)*

WILL. Oh, Mother!

HELEN. Happy!

*(*MRS. CROSBY *crosses to* HELEN, *pats her hand and stands between* WILL *and* HELEN, R.C.)*

WILL. Shall we tell 'em all?

MRS. CROSBY Tell them? *(She laughs)* What do you think they are? Blind and deaf? It's been a perfectly wonderful dinner. You were so blind to everything but each other. Oh, Billy, I thought your father would have a fit.

HELEN. I thought he had an awful cold, he was coughing terribly.

MRS. CROSBY. Coughing? He nearly strangled, to keep from laughing. I told him I'd send him from the table if he laughed at you.

WILL. Why, you never spoke to him once.

MRS. CROSBY. *(Between* HELEN *and* WILL, C.) Child, explain to him that wives don't have to—— Oh, I forget you haven't learned that yet. You know, Billy, I can talk to your father very effectively without words. *(Cross below table* R.)

HELEN. *(Turning to* MRS. CROSBY) Mrs. Crosby——

WILL. Mother, Nell's all fussed up because we've got money. She thinks you'll think—I'm—what in novels they call marrying beneath me. *(He and* MRS. CROSBY *laugh.* NELL *looks a little hurt.)*

HELEN. Well, he is.

MRS. CROSBY. Nonsense, child, don't be silly. *(Sits down stage end of table.)*

HELEN. *(To* MRS. CROSBY *a step)* It's not silly,

MRS. CROSBY.   Everyone will say it, and they'll be right.

WILL.   Let's settle this thing now once and for all, then.   In the first place it's all nonsense and in the second it isn't true——

HELEN.   Oh, yes it is.

MRS. CROSBY.   Oh, the first row!   I'll settle this one.   Nelly!

WILL.   Now then, Nell, out with it, get it all out of your system.

HELEN.   *(Xes to table* R. *a step)*   In the first place; it's the money.

MRS. CROSBY.   *(Seated below table* R.)   Yes, but —Helen——

HELEN.   Please, let me say it all.   You have social position, great wealth, charming friends, everything that makes life worth——   Oh, what's the use?   You know as well as I do the great difference between us, and——

MRS. CROSBY.   My dear child, suppose we admit all that, what then?

HELEN.   But don't you see——

WILL.   *(Embracing her in front of table* R.)   You little idiot!   I don't see anything but you.

MRS. CROSBY.   That's the whole of it, children. You love each other, suppose you listen to an old woman.

WILL.   Old!   Huh!

MRS. CROSBY.   *(Seated at table* R.)   Well, old enough.   Well, if Billy was the usual rich man's son, it might be different.   There might be something in what you say.   But, thank God, he isn't. Mind you, I don't say he wasn't like most of them when he was younger.   I dare say he was.   I know he went to supper with a chorus girl once.

WILL.   Twice.

HELEN.   What was she like?

WILL.   Like a chorus girl.

MRS. CROSBY.  The trouble with you, my dear, is that you've been reading novels.  When Billy's father married me, I was a school teacher, and he was a clerk.  We didn't have any money, but we were awfully in love—we still rather like each other. Now, just for the sake of argument.  Suppose we should have acted like stern parents, what would be the use?  Billy's in business for himself, he's making his own money, he can marry when he wants to and as he wants to, and if you want my real opinion, I don't mind confessing that I think he's pretty lucky to get you.

WILL.  There!

HELEN.  *(In front of table R.)*  But you know so little about me.

WILL.  Oh, rot.

MRS. CROSBY.  Thank you, Billy, I was trying to think of an effective word. *(To WILL.  To HELEN)* You've been my private secretary for over a year, and no matter how much my looks belie it, I'm not a bit of a fool.  I know a great deal about you.

HELEN.  My family——

WILL.  *(C.)*  I'm not marrying your family!

HELEN.  I'm afraid you are.

WILL.  Oh!

HELEN.  There's only mother.

MRS. CROSBY. *(Contritely, rises to HELEN in front of table R.)*  Oh, my dear, forgive me.  Your mother should have been here to-inght.

HELEN.  No, my mother—Mrs. Crosby—mother doesn't go out—she'd be unhappy here, and you'd be uncomfortable if she came.  You'll find her trying sometimes, you'll think she's common.  Oh, don't misunderstand me.  She's the most wonderful mother in the world.  And she's——

MRS. CROSBY.  Suppose, my dear, that we take your mother for granted—— *(Cross between WILL and HELEN)*  Take us as you find us and we will try to be happy. *(Enter* CROSBY *from door* L. *He is a fine-looking man of about sixty, with a pleasant personality, a good deal of charm and that masterful self-possession which sometimes marks the man of affairs. It is always evident that the most delightful intimacy exists between himself and his wife)* Well, Roscoe?

CROSBY. *(Cross to* L.C.—*takes* HELEN, *who crosses to* CROSBY, *in his arms)* Welcome, my dear.

HELEN. Oh, Mr. Crosby—I——

CROSBY. *(Placing* HELEN L. *of him with arms still around her—reaching his other hand to* WILL*)* Bill, shake! *(Father and son shake hands.* CROSBY *looks at his wife and they laugh gently)* Shall I tell 'em?

MRS. CROSBY. *(Standing in front of table over* R.*)* I would.

WILL. *(*R.C.*)* Tell us what?

CROSBY. *(*C.*)* You did this just in time. To-morrow I was going to forbid you to have anything more to do with this young woman.

HELEN. *(*L. *of* CROSBY*)* You see!

WILL. What for?

CROSBY. Your mother and I felt that you were pretty slow with your love-making.

WILL. Oh, Mother!

CROSBY. *(Continuing)* And I know darned well that if I interfered, you'd take the girl out and marry her.

HELEN. Oh!

WILL. You old schemer.

CROSBY. *(Crossing over* R.C. *below* MRS. CROSBY*)* I bet it would have worked.

WILL. *(As* CROSBY *crosses right,* WILL *slaps him on the back)* It would. *(Cross back of* HELEN *to* L.C.*)*

*(Door down* L. *opens and* EDWARD WALES *enters.)*

WALES.  I came ahead of the others to tell you——

CROSBY.  Why, Ned, old man, you came just in time to congratulate them.  *(He points toward* WILL *and* HELEN.)

WALES.  On what?  *(L.C.)*

MRS. CROSBY.  They're going to be married; isn't it fine?

WALES.  Oh!  *(There is a long pause.)*

WILL.  You haven't congratulated us, Mr. Wales.

WALES.  No, Will, I haven't.  I'm not sure that I can.  *(Down stage a step.)*

CROSBY.  Why, Ned!

WILL.  I'm afraid that calls for an explanation, sir.

WALES.  Yes, I expect that it does.  *(There is a long pause.)*

WILL.  Well?

WALES.  I'm sorry, but I can't explain anything until to-morrow.

MRS. CROSBY.  But really, Mr. Wales, don't you think——

WALES.  I think my action is almost indefensible.  I'm admitting that.  But I have very good reasons for what I am doing.  *(He turns to* CROSBY*)* Roscoe, I've been your close friend for a great many years.  You've trusted me, believed in me.  I'm going to ask you to wait.  After all, twenty-four hours can't make any difference, and it may save you all a great deal of unhappiness.

WILL.  *(Coming to* WALES *a step)* Why, this is intolerable.

CROSBY.  Ned, I can't understand——

WILL.  Father, this is my affair.

WALES.  I'm sorry.

WILL.  Sorry?  I should think you would be.

HELEN.  Billy, I told you what would happen.

Mr. Wales, I don't know what you have discovered, but it's nothing of which I am ashamed, nothing.

WILL. Dear, you mustn't mind what he says.

HELEN. *(In front of* WILL—*crossses to* WALES *a few steps)* Oh, but I do, I can't bear it. Why, my mother is the most wonderful woman in the world. I won't have her attacked. Do you know what she did? When I was ten years old she sent me away from her. I was the one thing she had in the world to love and she gave me up because she thought—because she thought it was the best thing she could do for me. I was sent to a fine school, then to college, and then when I was nineteen, quite by accident I found out that she wasn't dead, as they'd always told me, and when I went to her all she said was, "Well, my dear, I wanted to make a lady of you." *(Crosses to* WILL—C.—*He takes her in his arms, then* HELEN *crosses to* R. *of him.)*

MRS. CROSBY. *(In front of table* R.*)* I think she succeeded, my child.

WALES. *(*L.C.*)* Miss O'Neill, I didn't even know that you had a mother.

WILL. *(*C.*)* Then you'd better tell us now what ever your objection is.

WALES. I can tell you nothing until to-morrow. *(He turns to* WILL*)* Billy, I'd rather be shot than do what I'm doing. If I'm wrong I'll come to you gladly and eat dirt. I'll beg this young lady's pardon on my knees if she likes. *(Voices and laughter heard down* L.*)* Now that's all I'm going to say about it until then. *(Crosses up* L.*)*

*(The door at* L. *opens.*—EASTWOOD, HELEN TRENT, MISS ERSKINE, MISS STANDISH, STANDISH, MASON, *enter laughing and talking.)*

EASTWOOD. *(At* L.C. *To crowd in doorway)* And he said whose wife? *(All laugh.)*

WILL. (c.—HELEN *in front of table* R.) Quiet, quiet, everybody, I've got a surprise for you. (*People at door ad lib. laugh and buzz*) Nellie and I are going to be married.

(GIRLS *rush up* C. *and congratulate* HELEN—MEN *and* WILL *go to* L.C. *ad lib., business congratulating him.*)

MISS EASTWOOD. (*Coming to* WILL, C.) If you hadn't been engaged to her, she could have you arrested for the way you made eyes at her at dinner, Billy. But, of course, if people will marry— why—— (*She turns away* R. *from them*) I hope you will be awfully happy. (*Crosses to* MR. *and* MRS. CROSBY *down* R.)

MISS ERSKINE. (*Coming to* WILL) Isn't it beautiful? (*Crosses to* L.—*to settee.*)

MRS. TRENT. (*Crosses to* WILL, *kissing him*) I'm glad, Billy, glad. (*Cross to* STANDISH, *come down* L.—*and* TRENT *over* L.—MISS STANDISH *cross to front of table* R. WILL *and* HELEN *look around—see that no one is paying attention to them* —WILL *sneaks up to door* R.C.—*opens it—he and* HELEN *exit door* R.C. *quickly.* MRS. CROSBY, MR. CROSBY, EASTWOOD, *in front of table over* R. TRENT, STANDISH, MRS. TRENT, MASON *talking together over* L. WALES *up* L. *Ad lib conversation until* MISS EASTWOOD *speaks.*)

MISS EASTWOOD. (*To* MRS. CROSBY) Marriage is such an awful gamble. I know a girl who tried it four times. Billy, I hope you—— (*Turning to* C.) Why, they are gone.

(*Ad lib laughter of buzz and conversation.* MISS EASTWOOD *runs up to door* R.C., *opens it—looks in dining-room—gives a scream—closes door quickly, comes down to* R. *end of settee.* TRENT,

*to console table L. of settee, gets cigarette, lights
it. Crosses to C. back of settee in front of fireplace. STANDISH and MRS. TRENT to table L.
of settee. WALES and ERSKINE sit on settee
facing audience up C. MRS. CROSBY—at upper
end of table R. CROSBY seated R. end of settee,
facing audience up C.—MASON L. end of settee,
faces audience C. Enter BUTLER from down L.)*

BUTLER. Mrs. Crosby, the person you sent the
car for has arrived.

*(ALL turn eagerly toward the door L.)*

WALES *(Rises—goes to front of armchair L.C.)*
Can we see her now, Mrs. Crosby?

MRS. CROSBY. Certainly—Pollock, ask Madame
La Grange if she will come in, please.

BUTLER. Yes, Madame. *(He exits and closes
the door after him.)*

MISS EASTWOOD. *(Coming between table and
settee R.C.)* I'm perfectly thrilled. Do you suppose
she expects to be taken seriously?

MISS ERSKINE. Of course.

MISS EASTWOOD. *(At table R.)* How funny! If
you don't laugh at her, we can have no end of fun.
I'll guy her terribly and she'll never know it in the
world.

MRS. CROSBY. *(At table R.)* Oh, I wouldn't do
that, Mary. She may be quite in earnest.

MISS EASTWOOD. Oh, I can't believe that.
Madame La Grange! I can see her now. Tall, black-
haired creature, regular adventuress, see if she isn't.
Isn't she, Mr. Wales?

WALES. *(In front of settee)* She's the most re-
markable woman I have ever known.

*(Enter BUTLER from door L., coming well on stage.)*

Butler.    Madame La Grange.

*(Enter* Madame Rosalie La Grange. *She is a lit-tle Irish woman of about fifty, but old for her age. She is dressed quaintly. As she comes well on stage she stands and drops a little curt-sey.)*

Rosalie.    Good evenin', all av yes.

*(*Men *all rise.)*

Mrs. Crosby.    How do you do, Madame La Grange?
Rosalie.    I'm well, thank ye, ma'am.
Mrs. Crosby.    Won't you come in?
Rosalie.    I will, ma'am. *(She sees* Wales l.c. *and goes to him)*  Good evenin' to ye, Misther Wales.  Sure it was a grand hack ye sent for me.
Wales.    We all wanted you to be comfortable.
Rosalie.    Sure, an' I was. *(She laughs and turns to* Mrs. Crosby r.c.*)*  Do ye know, ma'am, when the gintleman in uniform come for me, I thought at first it was th' police.
Mrs. Crosby.    I hope you weren't frightened.
Rosalie.    *(*c.    Crosby r. *end of settee* c.—Mrs. Trent *and* Standish *move down* l., Trent *comes to* l. *of armchair—*Erskine *seated on settee up* c.—Mrs. Crosby *at table* r.    Wales l.c., Trent *and* Mason l.c.*)*  Divil a bit.  Sure I'd like to see the cop that could frighten me.  They're nice boys, thim cops, and most of thim good Catholics.
Miss Eastwood.    *(To* r. *side of* Rosalie*)*  Mr. Wales tells us you are wonderful.
Rosalie.    I am that.  Anny woman is.
Miss Eastwood.    *(With a meaning glance at the others)*  So you tell fortunes?
Rosalie.    No, miss, I do not.  I get messages

from thim that have passed on. I don't hold at all
wid the cards nor tea leaves nor any of thim tricks.
*(ALL laugh—*EASTWOOD *loudest)* Wance in a while
I give advice. *(She turns to* MISS EASTWOOD*)* If
I was you, Miss, I wouldn't meet Jimmy at the Ritz
at three to-morrow. *(ALL laugh.* MISS STANDISH
*crosses to settee* C. *Sits.* MISS ERSKINE *rises,
crosses to table* R.—*and sits in armchair.* MASON
*crosses—sits on up stage settee—*TRENT *to* L. *end
of settee—*MISS EASTWOOD *in front of table* R.
ROSALIE *goes to* WALES L.C., CROSBY *seats* MRS.
CROSBY *down stage end of table* R., *then crosses
back of* ERSKINE *to upper end of table)* Well, sor,
and how are ye?

WALES. We're expecting great things from you
to-night, Madame La Grange.

ROSALIE. Are ye now? Well, I hope ye won't
be disappointed.

CROSBY. *(Above table* R., *coming* C. *a step)* I
suppose there are a lot of tricks that——

ROSALIE. *(Interrupting him)* You said it, sor.
But I suppose mine is the only trade in the world
there's anny tricks in.

MISS EASTWOOD. *(Coming to* ROSALIE, *who is*
C.*)* Why shouldn't I meet Jimmy at the Ritz to-
morrow?

ROSALIE. If you do, sure, something awful is
liable to happen to him.

MISS EASTWOOD. What?

ROSALIE. Sure if you keep meeting the man he
is liable to marry ye. *(*EASTWOOD *up stage a step.)*

CROSBY. *(Upper end of table* R.*)* Would you
mind telling me how you know this young lady was
going to meet Jimmy at the Ritz to-morrow afternoon?

ROSALIE. I would not. Sure she left his letter
in her bag in the hall, and while I was waitin' I
read it.

MISS EASTWOOD.   How did you know it was my
bag?  *(c.)*

ROSALIE.   Sure, the stuff on the bag matches the
stuff on your dress.

MRS. CROSBY.  *(Seated below table R.)*  Then it
is all trickery?

ROSALIE.   It is, ma'am, and it ain't.  I tell ye,
ma'am, most of the time it's tricks, with even the
best of us.  But there's been times in my life when
—well, ma'am, thim times it wasn't tricks.  There's
been things I couldn't understand myself, messages
from thim that's passed on.   There is a power—a
wonderful—power—that comes to us.  But the divil
of it is ye never can tell when it's comin'.  Sure, if
ye waited for it ye'd starve to death.  So when it
ain't there we use tricks.

MRS. CROSBY.  *(Seated at lower end of table at
R.)*  I think I understand.

ROSALIE.   Do ye know, ma'am?  Well, do you
know, maybe I thought ye would.  *(Puts hand bag
on table R.)*

*(MRS. TRENT seated below door down L.  WALES
crosses down L. and joins MRS. TRENT at door
L.  CROSBY above table R.C.)*

MISS EASTWOOD.  *(Coming down to R.C.)*  Don't
you think all this is dishonest?

ROSALIE.  *(In front of table R.  Turning to her)*
What's dishonest?

MISS EASTWOOD.   Tricking a lot of poor, ignorant
people.

*(MASON back of settee C.)*

ROSALIE.   It's all in the way ye look at it.  A
widdy woman came to me this mornin' wid a breaking heart for the man that was gone.  I went into

trance and Laughing Eyes, me spirit control, came
with a message from him. Sure, she said he was in
Heaven wid the angels, and there was no cold nor
hunger; and the streets was paved with gold, and
there was music and happiness everywhere. She
told her he was thinkin' of her every day and every
hour and watchin' and waitin' fer the day she'd
come to him. Sure, wasn't that worth fifty cents
of any woman's money? The man may have been
in hell for all I know.

TRENT. *(By armchair* L.C.*)* What I can't understand is why you are telling us all this.

*(*MISS EASTWOOD *to settee* C. ROSALIE *to armchair*
L.C.*)*

MRS. TRENT. *(Seated over* L. *by door)* If we
know you are fooling——

ROSALIE. Didn't Mr. Wales tell ye?

WALES. *(*L.C.*)* I've told them nothing.

*(*MASON *drops down* R. *of settee.* STANDISH *down*
L.—CROSBY *is* R. *end of settee* C.*)*

ROSALIE. *(*C.*)* Well, tell thim now, plaze sur.
*(Sits upper end of table—takes off gloves, takes out
glasses from bag.)*

WALES. *(Down* L.*)* As I told you some time
ago, Madame La Grange has done a lot of things
that we can't explain.— When I asked her to come
here to-night, she said she would under certain conditions.

MASON. *(Between settee and table)* You mean
test conditions?

WALES. Not exactly. What she said was that
no money should pass between us, and that whatever she did, she would be honest.

MASON. *(Very eagerly)* You mean that you
won't play any tricks?

ROSALIE. *(Whisper.* MASON *comes to her, upper end of table* R.*)*  Av I do I'll tell ye.

MISS EASTWOOD. *(Seated on settee* C.*)*  Of course we understand all about spirit rappings.

ROSALIE.  Do ye now?

STANDISH. *(Down* L.*)*  Well, rather.

ROSALIE. *(*CROSBY *sits* R. *end of settee)*  Well, well, what do ye think av that?

MISS EASTWOOD.  You have to be near a table or something like that and——

ROSALIE.  Maybe a chair or a desk would do?

MISS EASTWOOD.  And then in the dark——

ROSALIE.  Av course in the dark.  And ye got wan rap for yes and two for no. *(There is a short pause.* ROSALIE *comes down* C.—*stands and says)* Are those spirits near? *(*ALL *laugh.)*

STANDISH.  Oh, no, don't.

ONE RAP

*(One rap is heard—from back of fireplace.  Little laugh.)*

MISS EASTWOOD.  But—— *(Rises, comes down* L.C. *a step.)*

MASON.  Oh, please keep still—— *(*ALL *gather a little closer around* ROSALIE.*)*

ROSALIE.  Is it Laughing Eyes?

*(One rap is heard—still louder)*  ONE RAP

And ye can't talk to me in the light?

*(One rap)*  ONE RAP

Are ye happy? *(*MRS. TRENT *rises)*

*(Two raps again)*  TWO RAPS

Is there someone here ye don't like?

*(One rap)*  ONE RAP

A gentleman?

*(Two raps)*  TWO RAPS

Dear, dear, a lady.

*(One rap)*  ONE RAP

*(She points to* MISS EASTWOOD*)* Is it that one?
*(One rap)*                              *ONE RAP*
Laughing Eyes don't like you. *(General laugh.)*

MASON. *(R.C.)* That's the most wonderful
thing I ever heard.

STANDISH. *(Down L.)* Oh, I don't think——

MASON. It couldn't be a trick. She just stood
there. I watched her hands every minute.

ROSALIE. Sure, ye watched the wrong end of me.
I have a wooden sole in me shoe. *(She lifts her
skirt and shows that she has taken one foot from
her slipper)* Ye do it with yer foot. Like this.
*(*TRENT *goes up to armchair* L.C. *Laughingly)*
Sure, it's a trick.

*(*MISS EASTWOOD *goes to* WALES L.C. MRS. TRENT
    *crosses up to armchair* L.C. STANDISH *crosses
    up to* L. *end of settee,* CROSBY C. MRS. CROSBY
    *seated at table* R. STANDISH *crosses back of
    settee to* R.C.*)*

MASON. Then if we get any messages——
*(*R.C.*)*

ROSALIE. If ye get any messages. Well, sur, I'm
tellin' ye the truth now. Most of the time it's fake.
With me, or that dago Palladino, and it was with
Slade, and all the rest of the trance mediums. But
to-night there'll be no fakin'. *(Rises)* I'm a
stranger to all of yez except Mr. Wales. I don't
know who lives in this house, I don't know the name
of any one of ye. Mr. Wales told me he wanted me
to come here, he said he'd be sendin' for me. He
ain't told me one word about any of ye. *(Goes to*
R. *end of settee.)*

WALES. That is quite true. *(Over* L.*)*

TRENT. *(By armchair* L.C.*)* You haven't given
her a hint of any sort?

WALES. *(L.)* On my word of honor.

MASON. *(Above table R.)* Madam La Grange?

ROSALIE. Sor?

MASON. I know a man who saw this woman Palladino lift a table just by putting her hands on it.

*(ROSALIE points to a small console table R. end of settee—it has a lamp on it—EASTWOOD L. end of settee.)*

ROSALIE. *(Putting handbag on chair above table R.)* Will some one please take the lamp off that table? And will you bring it here to me? *(MISS STANDISH crosses R. to upper end of table R., takes lamp and holds it. MASON brings console table to ROSALIE down C.—wide side to audience—ROSALIE puts her hands on table with her thumbs under its edge and lifts the table and turns R. and L.)* You mean like that?

MASON. Yes, I suppose that was it.

ROSALIE. In the dark ye wouldn't hardly notice my thumbs. *(ALL laugh. MISS ERSKINE seated back of table over R.)* But it can be done, it can be done. I don't say I can do it in the light, but if ye want I'll try.

ALL. Oh, yes, yes, of course, please do, yes, yes.

MASON. You mean without any trickery?

ROSALIE. *(Getting back of console table. Turning table around—narrow side to entrance)* I mean like this. *(She places the tips of the fingers of both hands on the C. of the table and stands rigid for a few moments. No one speaks. ALL watch her with breathless interest. Slowly the table tips a little to one side, and then tips in the opposite direction. Then it slowly rises about a foot from the floor, and then drops suddenly and falls over. There is a long pause.)*

MASON.  *(R. of small table)*  Good God.
WALES.  *(L.C.  Quietly)*  What did I tell you?

*(There is a long pause, ALL turn towards ROSALIE
to see what she will do next.  MASON takes console table back to its place R. end of settee.
TRENT, MRS. TRENT, over L.  STANDISH and
CROSBY C.)*

ROSALIE.  *(C.)*  Now ye all know what I can
do, but I can trick ye, too; so ye'll have to take my
word for it that I won't.  I'm not makin' you any
promises.  I'll go into trance for ye, and it will be
a real trance and no fake.  My spirit controls a
little girl named Laughing Eyes.
CROSBY.  *(Coming C.)*  Are you asking us to believe that the spirit of a dead child——
ROSALIE.  *(C.)*  To them that believes there is
no death.  Glory be to God, your own religion
teaches ye that.
CROSBY.  But not that the spirits of the dead can
come back to earth.
ROSALIE.  *(Goes to chair upper end of table—
CROSBY crosses to end of settee)*  Man, go read your
Bible.  *(STANDISH crosses to back of table R.)*  Sure,
I'm not going to argue with any of you.  I didn't
come here for argument.  Most of you don't believe,
you're all of little faith; sure, it's hard to get mes-
sages then.  Perhaps I'd better go about me business?  *(Crosses to L.C.)*
MRS. CROSBY.  *(At table R.)*  Oh, no, please stay.
ROSALIE.  Sure, ma'am, I'll be glad to.

*(WILL and HELEN enter R.C.  Cross down R.C.)*

TRENT.  *(Down L. of armchair)*  And you're
willing to submit to our conditions?
ROSALIE.  Of course, anything in reason—I——

HELEN. Why! *(Coming down* R.C.*)*

*(*ROSALIE, *at the sound of a new voice, turns. She
gives a little start, and then moves quickly to
HELEN—C.)*

ROSALIE. Wait, something's coming to me.
Don't anyone speak. *(*ALL *laugh. She goes close
to* HELEN *and looks at her—crosses down* C.*)* It's
a message—give me your hand, Miss. *(*HELEN, *in
a good deal of confusion, gives* ROSALIE *her hand.*
ROSALIE *stands and holds, her eyes are closed)*
Lady, there's nothin' but happiness comin' to you.
The spirits tell me you're the favorite child av fortune. *(*WILL *comes to* R.C.*)* You'll have wealth,
and prosperity, and happiness. You'll marry the
man you love, and ye'll be happy all your life long.
*(*WALES *goes up* L. TRENT *comes to* ROSALIE *a
step.* ROSALIE *turns to others)* There's something
I got to tell her, just fer herself it is. Sure, a young
girl like, it's her modesty I'm sparin'.

*(*MRS. TRENT *goes up* L. TRENT, EASTWOOD, *and
WALES goes up* L.C. ROSALIE *brings* HELEN
*down* L. WILL *joins* CROSBY *and* MRS. CROSBY
R.—ERSKINE *and* STANDISH *back of table* R.*)*

HELEN. Mother!
ROSALIE. Sure, darlin', I didn't know, they just
brought me here. Ye know I wouldn't have come
fer anythin' in the world. *(*HELEN *starts to break
away)* Don't tell them, dear, don't have me shame
you before all your fine friends. I'll go in a minute
—I'll get away the minute I can.
HELEN. But, Mother, there's no shame. I'm
proud——
ROSALIE. Tell them afterwards av ye must, but
let me get away first. *(Aloud)* Remember now,

Miss, all the love in the world is hangin' over ye, and prayin' for your happiness.  Don't let it go. *(Buzz—*ROSALIE *turns to* WALES L.  NELLIE *stands looking after her.* WILL *comes to her* R.C.*)*

WILL.  What did she tell you?

HELEN.  You heard most of it.  I'll tell you the rest later.  *(*WILL *and* HELEN *go up* R.C.*)*

ROSALIE.  I'm afraid I'd better go.

*(*EASTWOOD *and* TRENT *come down* L.*)*

WALES.  *(To the others)*  What do you think? Madame La Grange wants to call off the seance.

MISS EASTWOOD.  *(Down* L.*)*  I thought she might.

ROSALIE.  *(*MASON *above table* R.*)*  Did ye, now?

MRS. CROSBY.  Oh, won't you please stay?

*(*WILL *and* HELEN R.C.  MISS ERSKINE *above table* R.*)*

ROSALIE.  *(Comes* C.*)*  I'm afraid I can't, ma'am. I'm not feeling right, I ain't just meself.

WALES.  *(*L.C.*)*  Really, Madame La Grange.  I'm afraid under the circumstances.

ROSALIE.  *(Getting handbag from chair)*  I'm sorry but I got to go.

MISS EASTWOOD.  *(Down* L. *of* ROSALIE*)*  I think it's a shame to bother her.  And I think she's quite right to go.  Her sort of tricks aren't for people of intelligence.

HELEN.  Oh, won't you please stay?  *(To* ROSALIE C.*)*

ROSALIE.  I mustn't.

HELEN.  Won't you as a great favor to me?

ROSALIE.  Well, Miss, since you ask it.  I will stay.

*(Miss Eastwood laughs. She and Trent go up l.
Crosby by settee c. Mason below table r.
Mrs. Crosby seated lower end of table. Mrs.
Trent comes down to armchair l.c., sits.)*

Mrs. Crosby.    I'm very glad. Really, I'm greatly
interested.

Rosalie.    *(Crosses r.)*    Are ye now, ma'am?

Crosby.    *(To c.)*    I think after what we've seen,
that we must ask Madame La Grange to submit to
certain conditions.

Rosalie.    Anythin' at all, sur, anythin' at all.

Mason.    *(Down r.)*    I agree with you. Frankly
this woman impresses me.  I think this test should
be taken seriously.

*(Eastwood laughs.   Crosses to l. end of settee.)*

Wales.    *(l.c.)*    Just what I was going to say.

Crosby.    *(r.c.)*    If you will submit to the conditions we impose, Madame La Grange, and then show
us any manifestations, I will never scoff at anything
again.

Rosalie.    Sure, our scoffin's the easiest thing
any one can do.    *(Crosby crosses down r. below
table)*    If I could stop that even in one person, it
would be a good job.  What is it you want?

Crosby.    I want the window fastened.

Mason.    That's the idea.

Crosby.    *(Coming in front of table r.)*    Then
we will have the doors locked.  Will that be all
right?

Rosalie.    It will.

Miss Eastwood.    *(Coming down l.c.)*    At the
risk of seeming unnecessarily skeptical, I'm going
to suggest that we search Madame La Grange—that
is, of course, if she's willing.

*(Miss Erskine and Miss Standish back of
table r.)*

ROSALIE. *(c.)* Why not? There's no holes in
my stockings. *(All laugh.)*

MASON. *(Down r.)* I suppose it's going to be
difficult for you to get results if we are all so an-
tagonistic, Madame La Grange.

*(Miss Eastwood goes up l.c.)*

ROSALIE. Well, sur, it's up to them. If there's
any who wants to communicate with any here, maybe
they can reach us. I don't know. I don't understand ye. Sure, I showed ye all the tricks; would
I have done that, if I wanted to fool ye? I would
not. Then why won't ye give me credit for bein'
honest?

WALES. *(Down l. Ad lib buzz)* I'm sure
Madame La Grange is perfectly honest. We've made
certain stipulations to which she has agreed. I
think we've discussed matters enough already.
We're ready if you are, Madame La Grange.

ROSALIE. I'm ready.

*(Crosby looks at window fastenings.)*

MRS. CROSBY. *(Seated at table over r.)* Do you
know, I don't believe it will be necessary to subject
Madame La Grange to being searched. I'm quite
sure we can spare her that indignity.

ROSALIE. Sure, I don't mind if you fine ladies
won't be shocked at seeing plain, hand-sewed under-
wear.

*(Wales up l. Ad lib laugh. Erskine joining Will
and Helen, r.c.)*

MRS. CROSBY. *(Xing to* L. *of* ROSALIE C.*)* Come with me then, please.  I'm sure we won't be shocked. *(Aside to* ROSALIE*)* I wear that kind myself.

ROSALIE.  Do ye now, ma'am?  *(They go to door at* L.*)*

MRS. CROSBY. *(At door* L.*)* We sha'n't be long.

ROSALIE. *(At door* L.*)* Ma'am, would ye mind if all the ladies came?  Then they'll all be sure I ain't concealing nothing.

*(The* LADIES *all talk together and exit* L., *following* MRS. CROSBY.  WALES *closes door down* L.  CROSBY *comes to back of table* R.*)*

WILL. *(By table* R.*)* Do you really want that window fastened?

*(*STANDISH *back of chair below table* R.*)*

WALES. *(*L.C.  CROSBY *and* TRENT *sit on settee corner)* I don't care.

MASON. *(At table* R.*)* I'd like to make the test that way.  I've a queer feeling about that woman.  I believe she really has power of some sort.  I know it seems funny, but—well, you all saw her lift that table.  I watched her carefully.  There was no trick about it at all.  I'm sure of it.

CROSBY.  All right, then.  You fasten the window.  Billy, you and Brad go and get some chairs out of the dining-room, we'll need a lot.  *(*WALES *walks up and down* L. *stage.*  WILL *and* TRENT *exit door* R.C.*)* You put them in a circle, don't you? *(Begins to place chairs that are already in the room in a circle* C.*—armchair first* L. *of fireplace)* What are you going to do, Wales?  Ask her a lot of questions?

WALES. *(Over* L.*)* I'm going to try to find out who killed Spencer Lee.

CROSBY.    Still harping on the murder of Spencer Lee?

*(STANDISH places chairs above and below table in circle, then chair R. side of fireplace in circle.)*

WALES.    Yes.
MASON.    *(Over R., opening window curtains and raising windowshade)*  Who was Spencer Lee?
WALES.    The best friend I ever had.

*(TRENT and WILL enter door R.C., each carrying two chairs, bring them down R.C. and exit R.C.)*

STANDISH.    *(Placing chairs C. with backs to audience)*  We all knew Lee pretty well.  And I know he was no good.
WALES.    *(Crosses to L.C. outside of circle)*  You can't talk that way about him, Standish!
CROSBY.    *(In circle, comes down C.)*  The man's dead, why not let him rest in peace.

*(STANDISH outside of circle, L.C. seat.)*

STANDISH.    I didn't bring up the matter, you know, and I don't want to hurt Ned's feelings, but I know that the police found a lot of compromising letters and rotten things of that sort.

*(WILL and TRENT re-enter from R.C.  WILL crosses and places two chairs R. side of circle—closes door.)*

WALES.    *(L.C.)*  I don't care what they found, or what anyone thinks of Lee, he was my best friend and if I can find out who killed him I'm going to do it.  It was a damned brutal murder, stabbed in the back, poor chap, with never a chance to fight for his life. *(Crosses over* L.*)*

MASON. *(By table* R.*)* I don't seem to remember anything about the case.

WALES. It happened before you got back from France—no, by Jove, it didn't either. It was a day or two after. I remember you and I had lunch together the day you got home, and I had dinner that night with Spencer. Funny you don't remember anything about it.

(WILL *sitting* R. *in circle.*)

MASON. Well, of course, I must have seen it in the papers, but I don't go in much for crimes, and not knowing the man I wasn't interested.

STANDISH. *(Sitting in circle* L.C.*)* It was a good deal of sensation. The man knew a lot of nice people. Came here a good deal, didn't he, Mr. Crosby?

CROSBY. *(Sitting in circle up* C.*)* At one time. But after Helen married he rather dropped out of it. Fact is until Trent here appeared on the scene, he was always hanging around.

(TRENT *comes down and sits in* R. *side of circle.*)

STANDISH. Funny they never found out who killed him.

WALES. *(Standing outside of circle,* L. *side)* They may yet. They haven't stopped trying.

MASON. *(Seated on table* R.*)* Oh, are the police still interested?

WALES. Yes, they're interested. As a matter of fact, there's a reward of five thousand dollars for the discovery of the murderers.

STANDISH. Are you sure of that?

WALES. I offered it.

TRENT. You?

WALES.  Yes.  What sort of a man do you think I am?  Do you expect me to sit still and let the murderers of Spencer Lee go free?  Why, I'd known the man all his life.  We were the closest kind of friends.

WILL.  But if he was the kind of a man that Standish says——

WALES.  I don't give a damn what he was.  He was my friend and I'm never going to rest till I find out who killed him.

TRENT.  But——

WALES.  I wouldn't care so much if they'd given the poor devil half a chance for his life, but they stabbed him in the back.

MASON.  Wasn't there any indications——  *(Sitting on table R.)*

WALES.  *(Standing upper L. side—outside of circle)*  There wasn't a thing to show who did it or how it was done.  A knife wound between the shoulder blades and no knife ever found.  Nothing stolen, nothing disturbed.  The police have found out that a young woman called to see him that afternoon, two or three hours before his body was discovered.  That's all that we know.

TRENT.  *(With a laugh—still seated in circle)*  And now you're going to try spiritualism?

WALES.  Why not?  *(There is a pause)*  Do any of you object?

TRENT.  Certainly not.  I'm rather for it.

MASON.  *(Rises.  Still at L. table)*  You are doing this seriously?  This is not a joke?

WALES.  Quite seriously.  *(There is a pause)*  Well, why don't somebody laugh?

CROSBY.  My dear fellow, why should anyone laugh?  This queer old woman may have powers of which we know nothing at all.  Personally, I haven't much belief in that sort of thing, but I'm not going to laugh at it.  *(Rises)*  Neither am I going to have any trickery, or if there is any I'm going to expose it.

WALES. *(Over L.)* That's perfectly fair.

CROSBY. You've been at her seances or whatever they call them before?

WALES. Yes.

CROSBY. In the dark?

WALES. Invariably.

CROSBY. I may want light. *(He turns to his son)* Billy, if I call for lights you give them to me. Don't wait for anything, understand?

WILL. Perfectly, Dad. *(WILL goes up to small table R. of settee. Brings table with lamp on it down to between chair and his chair in circle.)*

CROSBY. That's all right, then. *(Still in circle. Door opens at L.—MRS. CROSBY enters, followed by MADAME LA GRANGE and other ladies. WALES crosses to R.C. outside circle. STANDISH crosses to upper end of table R. TRENT crosses to L. side of circle.)*

MRS. CROSBY. I think it wasn't fair to us.

ROSALIE. Sure, ma'am, I didn't mind.

*(MRS. CROSBY crosses back of settee to up R.C.)*

MISS EASTWOOD. *(Coming down L.)* I can assure you there isn't anything up her sleeve.

ROSALIE. Well, what did you expect, burglar's tools?

*(EASTWOOD goes up L. end of settee. HELEN and MRS. TRENT up L. MRS. TRENT closes door down L.)*

WALES. *(Over R.)* Madame La Grange, we've fastened the windows.

*(MISS STANDISH, MRS. TRENT, HELEN over L.*

Trent, Standish, Erskine *by console table* L. *of settee.)*

Rosalie. Have ye now?

Crosby. And now if you don't mind, I'm going to lock the doors and keep the keys in my pocket.

Rosalie. Anything at all, sir. Sure, it's all one to me. *(Goes inside circle and sits down* C. *in circle.)*

Mason. May I see that it's done, Mr. Crosby? *(*R.C.*)*

Crosby. *(*L.C. *With a laugh)* Can't you trust me?

Mason. It isn't that—I—well, I just want to be sure. To see for myself.

Crosby. Lock that one yourself, then. *(Indicating door* R.C. Crosby *goes to door at* L.C., *locks it, takes out the key and puts it in his pocket)* Better try it, Mason. *(*Mason *crosses to door* L.C.— *shows it is locked)* Now we'll do this one. *(He starts to door down* L. *Then stops suddenly)* No, I've got a better way than this. My dear, will you ring for Pollock?

Mrs. Crosby. *(Upper end of table* R.*)* What are you going to do now?

Crosby. Wait and see. *(To* Rosalie*)* You don't object to this?

Rosalie. I do not.

*(*Butler *enters from door* L.—*comes well on stage.)*

Crosby. Oh, Pollock, I want you to put these keys in your pocket. *(Hands them to him.* Pollock *puts them in his waistcoat pocket.* Mrs. Trent *and* Helen *down* L.*)*

Pollock. Yes, sir.

Crosby. *(*L.C.*)* Now then I want you to take

the key out of that door, and lock it on the outside, understand?

POLLOCK.    Perfectly, sir.

CROSBY.    Then take the key from the lock and put that one in your pocket also, after that you are to stand outside that door, and you are not to unlock it until I tell you to.   Understand?

POLLOCK.    Yes, sir, I'm to lock this door on the outside, keep the key in my pocket, and then stay just outside, and not open it for anyone until you tell me.

CROSBY.    Exactly.   *(Ad lib. buzz of conversation,* POLLOCK *goes to door* L., *takes out key, exits, closing the door after him.   The key is heard turning in the lock)*   Now then, Mason, you'd better try that door, too.   *(*MASON *goes over and tries the door* L. CROSBY *follows him.   Speaking through the door* L.*)* Are you there, Pollock?

POLLOCK.    *(Outside)*   Yes, sir.

CROSBY.    And the keys are in your pocket?

POLLOCK.    Quite so, sir.

CROSBY.    Now we're ready, Madame La Grange.

ROSALIE.    Then if ye'll all sit in a circle and hold hands.

ERSKINE.    Hold hands?   I'm going to love this. *(*ALL *laugh.)*

MASON.    *(Down to chair* L. *of circle)*   How shall we sit?   I mean do you want us in any particular order?

ROSALIE.    Any way at all.

MISS EASTWOOD.    *(*L. *to* ERSKINE, MRS. TRENT*)* And he said whose wife.

WILL.    I'll sit here.   *(Takes chair and sits in reach of lamp on table* R.C.*)*

ROSALIE.    Any way will do.


*(*HELEN *and* MRS. TRENT *come down* L.   *The* OTHERS *sit in a circle form the following order:*

ROSALIE, c.; CROSBY L. *of* ROSALIE; ERSKINE, MISS STANDISH, TRENT, MISS EASTWOOD, MASON, HELEN, MRS. TRENT, STANDISH *and* MRS. CROSBY. *This brings* WALES *sitting at* c. *with his back to the audience.* ROSALIE *directly opposite up stage, facing him. As they are being seated ad lib. buzz of conversation.)*

MISS ERSKINE. I'm to sit next to you, Mr. Crosby.

CROSBY. I've always wanted to hold your hands, my dear. *(Sitting in circle.)*

MRS. CROSBY. Don't trust him, Daisy. *(At* R. *of circle—sits in circle* R. *side.)*

MISS ERSKINE. I won't, Mrs. Crosby. *(Sits in circle.)*

MISS STANDISH. I'll chaperone them. *(Sits in circle between* TRENT *and* ERSKINE.*)*

MASON. *(To* HELEN*)* Will you sit by me? *(They sit in circle.)*

TRENT. I'll take this place, then. *(He sits in circle* L. *side.)*

MISS EASTWOOD. *(As she sits in circle)* I'm really getting quite a thrill. *(*ROSALIE *laughs)* What's the joke, Madame La Grange?

*(*MRS. TRENT *crosses outside of circle to* R.C. *and sits in circle.)*

ROSALIE. I didn't know anything could thrill you.

MISS EASTWOOD. You don't like me, do you, Madame la Grange?

ROSALIE. Sure, Miss, I'm crazy about you.

WALES. *(Standing below circle* R.C.*)* I think we're all ready. *(The* OTHERS *sit.* WALES *is about to sit.)*

ERSKINE. There are thirteen of us. Oh, don't

sit there, Mr. Wales. *(Counting hurriedly. She sits L. side of circle.)*

WALES. Oh, I don't mind those little superstitions. *(Sits down stage side of circle.)*

MRS. CROSBY. What do we do now?

*READY LIGHTS*

ROSALIE. I'd like for ye to join hands, and then sit quiet. Don't try to think of anything.

TRENT. By Jove, that'll be easy for me. *(The* OTHERS *laugh.)*

WALES. We can't get any results if you treat this as a joke. *(*ALL *laugh.)*

STANDISH. Oh, let's be serious.

MISS ERSKINE. Why, Howard!

STANDISH. Well, there might be something in it. Anyhow, it's only fair to do what Madame La Grange wants. I suppose you'd like the lights out? I've always understood that was necessary.

ROSALIE. We'll get better results that way.

*LIGHTS*

CROSBY. All right, then. *(He rises—goes to door* L., *pushes light switch below door L. This leaves only the two table lamps R. and L. of settee C. still lit. All other lights on scene out. Crosses back to his chair—turns out table lamp L.)* Will, you turn out that light as soon as we are ready.

*OUT*

WILL. Right you are, Dad.

ROSALIE. That's all, then. Sure, you're not to be frightened, if I cry or moan when I go into a trance. I'm not in pain or anything like that. I don't even know that I do such things, but I've been told that it sometimes happens. Me spirit control is a sweet little child, named Laughing Eyes. When she begins to talk ye can ask her anything you want. If she don't answer ye, she don't want to talk to ye. Then whoever's speaking had better let someone else

try it. That's all. *(She settles back in her chair)*
Now, thin, sir, ye can put out that light.

*(WILL turns off the light, and the stage is in darkness, all but spots on ceiling. House lights are all out, too.)*

CROSBY. That won't do. Billy, pull down the blind, that light on the ceiling is too strong.

*(WILL turns on lights. Crosses, pulls blind down, closes curtains, resumes his seat and puts light out. ROSALIE rises, crosses back of circle to back of MISS EASTWOOD's chair. There is a pause. Suddenly MISS EASTWOOD screams shrilly.)*

MISS EASTWOOD. There's a hand on my face, there's a hand on my face!
CROSBY. Lights, son!

*(The light on the table goes up, showing WILL leaning back in his chair with one hand on the switch, the other tightly clasped in his father's hand. ROSALIE is seen standing back of MISS EASTWOOD, with her hand resting on MISS EASTWOOD's cheek. All start to speak.)*

MRS. TRENT. It's a trick.
ROSALIE. Sure, it is a trick. *(They stop and stare at her. Her manner is commanding, and a little stern)* I was going to ask ye to tie me hands to the arm of the chair, but I thought I'd show ye this first.

MASON. I don't see how you did it—even now.
ROSALIE. *(Standing outside of circle L.)* Things happen in the dark. The sense of touch isn't much developed except ye're blind. When this young gen-

tleman let go my hand to turn out the light, I took my other hand away from Mr. Crosby and when we joined hands again the two gentlemen were holding hands as comfortable as you please. And I was free. It's an old trick. All the mediums use it. Anyone can do it. *(Back to her chair and sits)* Now, if someone will tie me in, we'll go on.

MASON. How do we know that you can't get free even then?

ROSALIE. Tie me so I can't.

CROSBY. *(Rising)* I'll see to that. I want something strong.

MASON. Take handkerchiefs, they are strong enough. *(Takes handkerchief.)*

CROSBY. They'll do very well. *(Takes out his own)* I want three more.

WILL. Here's mine. *(Hands his handkerchief to his father.* MASON *and* TRENT *give* CROSBY *theirs.)*

CROSBY. Now, Madame La Grange, if you don't mind. *(He goes, ties her hands to the arm of the chair)* I don't see why you did that just now.

ROSALIE. I told you I wanted to be sure.

CROSBY. Why?

ROSALIE. Because I think something's going to happen. I think there will be manifestations. I wanted you to know I wasn't faking.

MISS EASTWOOD. Why should we think that you were?

ROSALIE. Sure, ye thought nothing else since I came into the room.

CROSBY. Mason, see if she can get free from that now.

*(*MASON *comes over, inspects the knot,* CROSBY *tying the other hand.)*

MASON.   That seems pretty secure—someone esle look at it.

(WILL *and* TRENT *rise and go to* ROSALIE's *chair.*)

CROSBY.   I'm going to fasten your ankles now, Madame La Grange.
ROSALIE.   That's right.

(CROSBY *ties* ROSALIE's *ankles to leg of chair. The other two men look on.*)

WALES.   I don't believe all this is necessary.
ROSALIE.   Why not, if they want it?
CROSBY.   Now I'm sure she can't get away.   (MASON *inspects knot.*)
MASON.   So am I.   (*The men resume their places.*)
ROSALIE.   Well now, if ye'll all sit down, please— (*Pause*)—ye'll have to reach over and take my hands this time—are ye all satisfied now?   Is there anything more ye want me to do?   (*There is no answer*)   Then, if ye'll all sit quiet, just keep yer minds free, that's all ye have to do.   Now, sir, ye can turn out the lights.

*LAMP OFF*
(*There is a long pause.* ROSALIE *moans and whispers as if in pain.*)

HELEN.   I can't stand this, I——
WALES.   Please keep still—she asked us to keep still.

(ROSALIE *moans again.   After a short pause, she gives a choking sob.   Another pause.   Finally she speaks with frequent pauses, using the voice of a little child.*)

*SET*

ROSALIE. Laughing Eyes is sad, very sad. I'm a long way off—a long way. *(Pause)* Bad people, bad people, unhappy—he's unhappy—— *(Pause. Knife is set down in sight of audience, seen sticking in ceiling)* Spencer wants to tell Ned—— *(She moans heavily)* It hurts—terribly—like a knife—it burns—burns, in the back—— *(MAN'S voice from settee, facing fireplace, says)*

VOICE. Ned, I want Ned—why in *hell* don't Ned answer?

ROSALIE. *(In child's voice)* He wants to talk to Ned—is Ned here?

STANDISH. Ned who? Who is it? Who does he want to speak to?

ROSALIE. *(In child's voice)* Tell Ned it's Spencer—Spencer wants to tell Ned about the letters and the pain in the back—in the back.

STANDISH. What was in the back? *(There is no answer)* Ask him what was in the back!

ROSALIE. *(Still using child's voice)* The knife —Ned—he wants Ned.

WALES. What do you want?

ROSALIE. A swimming pool—don't forget the swimming pool. Don't ever forget——

WALES. You mean the time he went in after me when I was drowning? When we were little boys? Is that what he wants me to remember?

ROSALIE. Spencer says he can't rest—he wants to tell you it's hard to reach—too far away—you promised——

WALES. Promised what? When did I promise?

ROSALIE. Your life saved——

WALES. Now I know—I told him I'd do anything in the world for him. Spencer, of course, I remember—what do you want me to do?

ROSALIE. Find—find——

WALES. Do you want me to find the letters?

ROSALIE. In the back—someone came—someone came.

WALES. You're trying to tell who killed you?

ROSALIE. Ask—ask—ask.

WALES. You want me to ask questions? Is that it? You mean you can't talk much?

ROSALIE. Too far away.

*READY LIGHTS*

CROSBY. You know who killed you? *(There is a pause, but no answer.)*

ROSALIE. He says, Ned, he wants Ned.

WALES. You want me to ask?

ROSALIE. He wants Ned to ask.

WALES. Do you know who killed you?

MRS. TRENT. *(Hysterically)* Oh, my God!

CROSBY. Keep still, daughter.

WALES. Can you tell the name? (ROSALIE *suddenly gives a long moan)* Quick, the name, the name. Spencer, tell me who killed you—she's coming out of her trance. I want the name. (ROSALIE *moans again. Her cry is over-topped by a shriek from* WALES) Oh, my God. My back—Oh! *(Then there is a dead silence that lasts as long as it will hold.)*

CROSBY. Wales, is anything the matter?

MRS. TRENT. Father, he's pulling at my hand.

*TABLE LIGHT ON*

CROSBY. Lights, son.

*(WILL suddenly turns on the light at table. WALES is discovered leaning forward, the circle is unbroken.)*

MRS. TRENT. Look at him! Father! Look at him!

*(CROSBY drops ROSALIE'S hand and springs forward toward WALES. At the same instant WALES*

*falls forward on his face to the floor. The
others all rise, chairs are knocked over in the
confusion which follows.)*

*WARN*

CROSBY. Stand back, please. *(The OTHERS move
back a little—CROSBY leans over WALES)* Why, he
—why—it's impossible.

MRS. CROSBY. Roscoe. look at your hand.

*(CROSBY looks at his hand, takes out his handker-
chief and wipes it hurriedly. He crosses suddenly to the door at L. ROSALIE has come out
of her trance and sits staring at WALES as he
lies on the floor in front of her. The two fig-
ures are thrown out from the shadows of the
room by the light on the table back of MADAME
LA GRANGE. The rest of the room is in semi-
darkness.)*

CROSBY. *(TRENT kneels by WALES' body)* Pollock! Pollock!

POLLOCK. *(Outside)* Yes, Mr. Crosby. *(TRENT
turns WALES' body over on back.)*

CROSBY. Get on the phone at once and call up
Police Headquarters. Get Inspector Donahue if you
can. Tell him to come to the house at once.

*READY CURTAIN*

POLLOCK. Very good, sir.

*(CROSBY turns away from the door, and faces the
OTHERS, who have followed him over.)*

WILL. Father, what do you suppose it is? Are
you sure that——

MRS. TRENT. It can't be. He was talking
and——

Mrs. Crosby.   Roscoe, are you sure?   Hadn't we better send for Doctor Griggs?

*(Trent is leaning over Wales' body on floor.)*

Trent.   It's no use.   He's dead.

Crosby.   Murdered.

Trent.   *(Rises)*   What?

Crosby.   Mr. Wales was stabbed in the back, just as Spencer Lee was stabbed in the back.

Standish.   Just as he was asking—just when he was trying to find out who——

*(There is a knock on the door down L.)*

Crosby.   What is it?

Pollock.   *(Outside of door)*   Inspector Donahue was at the Fifty-first Street Station, sir.   He's on his way here.   *(There is a pause)*   Shall I unlock the door, sir?

Crosby.   *No*—not until the Inspector tells you.

## CURTAIN

# ACT II

SCENE:  *Same as Act I.*

TIME:  *Ten minutes later.*

DISCOVERED:  CROSBY *is standing by door* L.  ROSA-
LIE *is still tied in chair.  Dummy supposed to
represent* WALES' *body covered by a piece of
drapery, has been placed on settee facing fireplace up* C.

MRS. TRENT *seated below console table* L. *end
of settee.*

MISS EASTWOOD *seated next to* ROSALIE *at* R.
*end of console table* R. *of settee.*

STANDISH *over* R. *by table.*

HELEN *and* WILL—*standing above table* R.

MRS. CROSBY *seated* L., *next to* ROSALIE.
MISS ERSKINE *seated next to* MRS. CROSBY.
MASON *in front of fireplace* C., *looking at*
WALES' *body.*

TRENT *walking up stage* L. *as curtain rises.
All lamps on stage lit.  Rose foots up full.
Amber foots one-quarter up.  No border light.*

*Arrangement of chairs for Second Act.  Big
armchair up* C., *facing audience.  Single chair*
R. *of armchair.  Chair upper end of table* R.
*Armchair back of table* R.  *Chair lower end of
table* R.  *Small chair in front of table* R.  *Small
chairs down* C., *with space between; these two
chairs turn sideways to audience.  Chair down*
L.  *Armchair against flat below door* L.  *Chair
up* L.  *Chair with upholstered seat* L. *of* ROSA-
LIE'S *chair.  Small chair* R. *corner of console
table,* L. *of settee.  Small chair* L. *side, a little*

*below console table* L. *end of settee.  Book on*
*table* R. *end of settee.  Console table moved up*
*stage to* R. *end of settee.* STANDISH *teetering*
*chair below table* R., ERSKINE *tapping chair,*
EASTWOOD *rattling book leaves.* MASON *takes*
*book away from her.* MISS STANDISH *sitting*
L.C. *between* MRS. CROSBY *and* MRS. TRENT.
*As curtain rises,* MRS. TRENT *rises, goes to*
CROSBY L.  TRENT *walks up stage* L. *at rise.*

MRS. TRENT.  *(Rises, goes* L. *to* CROSBY*)*  Father
please let me go to my room.
CROSBY.   It is impossible, my dear.
TRENT.   But, Mr. Crosby——  *(Goes to* CROS-
BY L.*)*
CROSBY.   *(Interrupting him)*  It's quite impos-
sible.

*(*MRS. TRENT *sits in chair up* L., *followed by* TRENT,
*who stands* R. *side of* MRS. TRENT.  STANDISH
*is standing by table over* R.*)*

STANDISH.   *(Below table over* R.*)*  Mr. Crosby,
I must——
CROSBY.   *(*WILL *sits back of table* R.  HELEN *sits
above table* R.*)*  Mr. Standish, I just refused to let
my own daughter leave the room.  *(Slight pause.)*
STANDISH.   But don't you see, sir——
CROSBY.   My dear Standish, poor Wales was
killed by someone in this room.  We are all of us
under suspicion.  Everyone of us.  *(Slight movement from* ALL*)*  It's an awful thing to say—someone of us in this room has killed Wales—which one
of us?

*(Knock on door down* L.*)*

*THREE KNOCKS*

CROSBY. Yes.

POLLOCK. *(Outside)* The police are here, sir.

CROSBY. Who is it?

DONOHUE. *(Outside at door down* L.*)* Inspector Donohue.

CROSBY. (WILL *rises)* Pollock, you will give Inspector Donohue all the keys.

POLLOCK. Yes, Mr. Crosby. *(There is a pause.)*

DONOHUE. *(Still outside the door)* What is all this?

POLLOCK. *(Outside door down* L.*)* I don't know, I'm sure. I was told to lock the door. I don't know what's been going on inside. Then I was told to call you. This is the right key for that door.

*(The noise of the key being put into the lock can be heard, then the click as it is turned in the lock, then the door is opened, and* INSPECTOR DONOHUE, *in citizen's dress, comes well on stage* L. SERGEANT DUNN *enters, drops below door* L. *He is seen to be a clean-cut, intelligent-looking man of fifty. It later develops that he is reserved and extremely quiet in manner. He speaks like a gentleman and acts like one. He is as little like the traditional stage police inspector as it is possible to induce a tradition-bound manager to permit.)*

DONOHUE. Oh, Wales! Where's Mr. Wales?

CROSBY. *(*L.C.*)* How did you know that Wales——

DONOHUE. *(*L. *of* CROSBY. *Interrupting him)* I don't know anything. I was thinking of something else. I was told that I was wanted here in a hurry.

CROSBY. Queer your asking for Wales. Mr. Wales is dead; that's why I sent for you.

DONOHUE. Wales is what?

CROSBY. Wales is dead.

MISS EASTWOOD. *(Still seated* R.C.*)* Yes, and if you ask me——

DONOHUE. Just a minute, please, Miss. *(He turns to* CROSBY*)* It must have been very sudden. Why, only this afternoon I—— Did he ask you to send for me?

CROSBY. *(*L.C.*)* Inspector, you don't seem to understand. Mr. Wales was murdered in this room not fifteen minutes ago.

*(Other characters keep positions as at rise of curtain.)*

DONOHUE. *(His manner changing abruptly)* Mike! That door! *(*SERGEANT DUNN *closes door* L. *and stands in front of it)* Where have you taken him?

CROSBY. *(Pointing to the sofa* C.*)* There.

*(*DONOHUE *goes up* L. *end of settee* C.*, stands looking down on the body. There is a long pause and then, slowly raising his head, looks with terrible deliberation at each person in the room.* MASON *goes to* R. *end of settee.)*

DONOHUE. Who did this?

CROSBY. We don't know.

DONOHUE. *(Very quietly)* Then I expect we'll have to find out. *(He comes down* R. *end of settee, stops when he sees* ROSALIE. *He gives a short laugh as he sees how she is tied to the chair)* What's this? *(*R.C.*)*

MRS. CROSBY. *(Rises)* Good Heavens, we forgot to untie her. I'm so sorry.

ROSALIE. Thank ye, ma'am, I'm quite comfortable as it is. I'll stay as I am if ye don't mind.

MRS. CROSBY. But—— *(Bus. unties.)*

DONOHUE.   I think we'll leave things as they are for the present.

*(*MRS. CROSBY *resumes same seat as before.)*

ROSALIE.   Bless me soul, a cop with brains!

DONOHUE.   *(Goes to* CROSBY *down* L., *standing* R. *side of* CROSBY*)*  Let's see if he can't use them then.   Now, Mr. Crosby, tell me exactly what happened.

CROSBY.   (L.C.)  I know it sounds foolish, but we were having a spiritualistic seance.   Madame La Grange is a medium.

DONOHUE.   I see.

CROSBY.   We were sitting in the dark, in a circle, you know, holding hands.   Suddenly Wales cried out.   I called to my son to turn on the light.   He did so.   Wales was leaning forward in his chair.   His hands were in those of the people he sat between, and all the rest of us were sitting around.

DONOHUE.   *(*R. *of* CROSBY*)*  All of you?

CROSBY.   Yes.

DONOHUE.   I thought you told your son to turn on the lights.   *(*L.C.*)*

CROSBY.   If you're implying that——

DONOHUE.   I'm not implying anything, and please answer my questions.

WILL.   *(Rises, and stands back of table* R.*)*  Why, Inspector, I was sitting there, and simply made a move to turn on the light.   I had chosen the seat purposely.   We wanted to expose trickery, if we found any.

DONOHUE.   I understand.   Go on, Mr. Crosby. *(He turns again to* CROSBY.*)*

CROSBY.   (L.C.)  In a moment poor Wales fell to the floor.   I ran to him and found that he had been stabbed in the back.   Before we could call for aid, he was dead.

DONOHUE.   Did he say anything?

CROSBY.   No.   I think that he was dead before we got to him.

DONOHUE.   What happened then?

CROSBY.   As soon as I realized what had happened, I sent for you.

DONOHUE.   Why for *me?*   Why not simply notify the police?   I mean, was there any special reason for wanting *me?*

CROSBY.   There was, but I wasn't conscious of it at the time.   We'd been talking about the killing of Spencer Lee earlier in the evening, and I suppose that subconsciously I remembered that you were handling that case, which brought yours as the first name to my mind.   That's all.

DONOHUE.   I see.   *(Goes to* C. *a few steps)* Now, then, who's been in or out of this room since? Of course you know you had no right to move Mr. Wales.

CROSBY.   *(*L.C.*)*   Yes, I know, but I couldn't let him lie there on the floor.   It was a little too much. You see, we were all locked in here and——

DONOHUE.   Locked in?   You mean as I found you when I came?

CROSBY.   Exactly.   We had all of the windows fastened and all doors locked for the seance.   Pollock had the keys.   I refused to let him open the door until you came.

DONOHUE.   Mr. Crosby, you are forgiven for breaking the Coroner's rules.   As I understand, then, you were sitting in this room with the doors and windows locked; you were in the dark, Wales was stabbed in the back, the lights were turned on, and no one has left the room or entered since?

CROSBY.   No one but you.

DONOHUE.   I didn't kill him.   *(Crosses* C.   *There is a long pause, then he turns with a sweeping gesture.)*   Which one of you did?   *(Slight movement from* OTHERS—*who are still seated. There is a long pause. No one speaks. Very quietly down* R.C. *Below table* R.) Now, I'm not going to employ the usual police methods. There is to be no bulldozing or threatening or badgering. But you all can see that there can be no escape for the guilty person. I realize that this is a terrible situation for all of you, but the only way to relieve it is for the murderer of Mr. Wales to confess. *(Another pause)* It will save a long, and I assure you, a very trying police investigation. Let me say also that there will be no recriminations, no unpleasant scenes. I realize that this seems a very weak plea for a confession. But I am counting on the intelligence of the people now in this room. *(He takes out his watch, and holds it face upward in his hand)* I have unlimited time. But not a great deal of patience. Well? *(There is another long pause. He finally replaces his watch with a little gesture of finality. He turns suddenly to* MISS EASTWOOD, *who is still seated up* R.C.) Very well, then. What is your name?

MISS EASTWOOD.    Mary Eastwood.

DONOHUE.    A moment ago, Miss Eastwood, you started to tell me something. You said "if you ask me." Now I am asking you. What was it you wanted to tell me?

MISS EASTWOOD.    *(Seated* R. *of console table* R.) I don't want to especially. But I think I ought to tell you this. No one else seems to have thought of it. When the seance started we were all sitting in a circle holding each other's hands. As I understand it——

DONOHUE.    We can take it for granted that I know how that is done. Go on, please.

MISS EASTWOOD.    The medium got out of the circle without our knowing it, and then showed us how she did the trick.

DONOHUE.    I see.

MISS EASTWOOD. Why couldn't she have done it again? Of course, that's what someone did, isn't it? And if she could get out of the circle, without our knowing it, she could get back in again, couldn't she? *(With an air of triumph—*HELEN *rises)* *That's* what I wanted to tell you.

ROSALIE. If anyone of ye or all of ye can get me out of this chair without untying me or cutting me loose, I'll say I done that murder.

*(*HELEN *sits above table* R.*)*

DONOHUE. Thank you, Miss Eastwood. It's only fair to tell you that there isn't a trick or an effect that these people do that the police do not understand perfectly.

ROSALIE. Is that so?

*(*DONOHUE *goes over and examines the way in which* ROSALIE *is tied to the chair.)*

DONOHUE. Why was she tied up?

CROSBY. *(Down* L.C.*)* At her own request. As Miss Eastwood says, she showed us how she broke out of the circle and then suggested that we tie her into that chair to make sure she didn't do it again.

DONOHUE. *(*R. *of* ROSALIE'S *chair)* It's lucky for her that she did. Even if she had gotten out of those knots, there's no way in the world that she could get back in.

ROSALIE. I said the cop had brains. *(*DONOHUE *turns away from her)* Get me loose, Inspector, dear, me foot's asleep.

*(*DONOHUE *turns back, unties handkerchief with which she is tied. She gets up and stands in front of armchair* C.*)*

DONOHUE. Thank you very much, Miss East-wood, that eliminates one.

ROSALIE. Then I can go? *(Starting for door* L.*)*

DONOHUE. You cannot. (ROSALIE *goes* R. *of armchair and sits* R. *end of settee* C.*)* Anyone else have anything they want to tell me? No? Mike, you'd better phone the Coroner and ask him to come up here. Tell him I do not want the case reported yet. And suggest that he hurries.

DUNN. Yes, Inspector. *(He turns and exits* L., *leaving the door open behind him.*—STANDISH *starts to door* L.*)*

DONOHUE. *(Turning to* STANDISH *and* TRENT— *who start to go* L.*)* That open door does not mean freedom for any of you yet.

TRENT. *(Coming to* DONOHUE C.*)* I'm awfully sorry, Inspector, but I've an important business engagement at ten o'clock. My father-in-law here will——

DONOHUE. That's quite impossible.

*(*TRENT *goes up* L. *again and stands* L. *side of* MRS. TRENT.*)*

STANDISH. *(Crosses* L.C.*)* This is all very well, Inspector, but you know you can't keep us in this room forever. If you want to take the consequences of accusing me of murder; well, that's your affair. But my patience is exhausted and I haven't the slightest intention of remaining here much longer. Unless, of course, you are planning to arrest me.

DONOHUE. I see. *(*C.*)* By the way, who are you?

STANDISH. *(*L.C.*)* Howard Standish, of Standish, Giles & Updegraff, 120 Broadway. My brother is Judge Standish of the Supreme Court.

DONOHUE. And you refuse to remain here any longer? *(*C.*)*

STANDISH.  I do.  *(L.C.)*

DONOHUE.  Very well, Mr. Standish, of Standish, Giles & Updegraff.  You are arrested as a material witness in this case.  As soon as Sergeant Dunn returns, he will call a patrol wagon and take you down to the House of Detention.  *(Turns—crosses R.)*  Are there any others who insist on leaving this room?

STANDISH.  *(L.C.)*  I beg your pardon, Inspector, I acted like a fool.  *(MASON R. of settee C.)*

DONOHUE.  Not at all, sir, your actions are entirely natural.

*(STANDISH goes up L.  DUNN's voice is heard outside.)*

DUNN.  Hello! Hello! No, sir.  But Inspector Donohue wants you to come here at once.  We're at Mr. Roscoe Crosby's house.  No, sir—*(DONOHUE crosses and closes the door L.)*—he doesn't want the case reported yet.

DONOHUE.  We needn't be bothered with that, anyway.  *(Crosses to R.C.  There is a pause)*  Well, I'm afraid we'll have to begin work.  *(He goes over to table R. and sits down stage end of table.  Takes paper, gets pencil)*  With the exception of Mr. Crosby, who is known to nearly every one, and Mr. Standish, who has so pleasantly introduced himself to me, I know none of you.  So I'll have to ask——  *(He stops suddenly and rises, facing them all.  He points slowly to the sofa, facing fireplace up C.)*  That's rather a gruesome thing there.  I think we'll move it into another room.  Will some of you gentlemen carry Mr. Wales' body into the other room?  *(There is a pause.  The MEN all hesitate.  Finally MASON starts to settee C. down stage R.C.)*  Thank you very much, we'll——  *(Coming to C.)*

*(DUNN enters from L.)*

DUNN.   Dr. Bernstein himself is on the way here, Inspector.

DONOHUE.   Good.  Mike, get one of the servants to help you to carry this sofa into another room. *(DUNN turns and exits L. without speaking)*  I won't have to trouble you after all, sir. *(MASON drops to console table R. of settee.  He gives a little laugh)*  Funny how these old superstitions cling to us.  One of the first tests for guilt invented by detectives was to ask a supposed murderer to touch the body of his victim. *(Slight pause)*  The test didn't work very well, did it?  Certainly you four gentlemen can't all be guilty. *(Slight pause)*  Well, we'll have to try something else. *(Very impressively)*  Because you know I really am going to arrest the murderer of Edward Wales to-night. *(DUNN enters from L., followed by POLLOCK)*  Carry the sofa into another room, please.

CROSBY.   *(Down L.)*   Into that room, please. *(Indicating door L.C.)*

*(DUNN goes up to door L.C., turns knob—discovers door is locked.  POLLOCK crosses to R. end of sofa, facing fireplace on which dummy has been placed between First and Second Acts.  Dummy is covered with a drapery.)*

DUNN.   *(At door L.C., the door is locked)*   The door is locked.

DONOHUE.   *(C.)*   Oh, yes, try these keys.

*(DUNN comes down L.C., gets keys, goes up and unlocks door.—He and POLLOCK pick up settee— POLLOCK taking his end of settee through door L.C. first.)*

DONOHUE.   And Mike——   *(DUNN turns his head.)*

DUNN. Yes, sir.

DONOHUE. Make as quick an examination as you can and report to me here. *(The* MEN *exit, carrying sofa into room* L.C. DONOHUE *crosses to chair below table* R.—*sits.* MISS STANDISH *sits in circle between* ERSKINE *and* TRENT. TRENT *places chair* L.C.*)* If you will all come a little closer, please. *(*WILL *back of table* R.—HELEN O'NEILL *seated above table,* MISS EASTWOOD *seated below console table* R. *end of settee,* ROSALIE *seated* C. *settee,* MRS. CROSBY *seated in armchair up* C., MASON *standing upper end of table* R., MISS ERSKINE *seated up* L.C. MRS. TRENT *seated,* STANDISH L. *of armchair, and* TRENT *seated* L.C. CROSBY *down* L.C.*)* Now I can see you all quite comfortably. *(Seated lower end of table* R. POLLOCK *enters door* L.C.*, closes door—crosses to door* L.—*Exits, closing door)* As I started to say a moment ago, I shall have to find out something about each of you. You, Madame? *(He turns to* MRS. CROSBY.*)*

MRS. CROSBY. *(Seated in armchair* C.*)* I'm Alicia Crosby. Mrs. Roscoe Crosby. *(He makes notes, with pencil on paper in front of him.)*

DONOHUE. I'm sorry to trouble you, Miss—— *(He points his pencil at* MISS ERSKINE, L.C.*)*

MISS ERSKINE. Elizabeth Erskine. I'm——

DONOHUE. It's not necessary to tell your age.

MISS ERSKINE. I wasn't going to. I'm the daughter of Edward Erskine. My father is the banker. *(Sits* L.C.*)*

DONOHUE. I know him. Thank you. You are then merely a guest here?

MISS ERSKINE. A friend.

DONOHUE. Miss Eastwood, I already know.

DONOHUE. And you, Miss?

MISS STANDISH. Grace Standish.

STANDISH. My sister.

DONOHUE. Oh! And this young lady?

CROSBY. *(He puts his hand on* MRS. TRENT'S *shoulder,* L.C.) My daughter, Mrs. Trent. She and Trent, here, live with us.

DONOHUE. And you, sir?

MASON. *(There is a pause)* Phillip Mason. *(At upper end of table* R.)

DONOHUE. That doesn't tell me very much.

MASON. *(With a laugh)* There isn't much to tell. I'm just a friend of the family's. We've known each other for years. I've lived in Paris for the last two or three years. I'm a painter.

DONOHUE. You mean an artist?

MASON. Well, I don't paint houses or fences, but I'd hardly call myself an artist—yet.

DONOHUE. Poor, I suppose? I know you'll pardon that question, won't you?

MASON. Quite all right, I assure you. No, I'm not poor.

DONOHUE. *(He turns toward* WILL *who is standing back of* HELEN'S *chair above table* R.) Thank you. And you?

WILL. I'm young Crosby.

DONOHUE. I see. Live home, I suppose?

WILL. Certainly, where else should I live?

DONOHUE. I thought perhaps you might be married.

CROSBY. *(*L.C.*)* He's not, but if he were he'd live with us and——

WILL. No, Father. When I marry I've got to have my own home and——

CROSBY. Nonsense. Don't talk like a fool. You'd live here with me and your mother—and your wife, of course.

DONOHUE. I think perhaps we'd better defer that discussion, gentlemen. *(He turns toward* HELEN*)* And this young lady?

WILL. My fiancée, Miss O'Neill.

DONOHUE. Well, that finishes that. *(Rises— stands below table* R.*)*

MISS EASTWOOD. But, Inspector, you haven't asked anything about the medium?

DONOHUE. Perhaps I don't consider that necessary, Miss Eastwood.

MISS EASTWOOD. But——

DONOHUE. And I'm terribly set on conducting this investigation in my own way, if you don't mind.

*(Enter DUNN from* L.C.*)*

DUNN. Inspector.

DONOHUE. Well?

DUNN. *(At door* L.C.*)* I can't tell for sure, but I guess the knife went clean into the heart. He must have died instantly.

DONOHUE. All right. Let me know when the Coroner arrives. *(DUNN turns and starts toward door down* L.*)* And Dunn!

DUNN. Yes, sir.

DONOHUE. *(Going* C.*)* You'd better let me have a look at that knife.

*(DUNN turns sharply and looks at him.)*

DUNN. *(Down* L.*)* The knife?

DONOHUE. Yes, the knife.

DUNN. I haven't seen any knife. I thought you had it.

DONOHUE. No. I haven't seen it. *(There is a long pause.* R. *of* CROSBY*)* Mr. Crosby?

CROSBY. *(Still* L.C.*)* We didn't find it.

DONOHUE. Look carefully?

CROSBY. Everywhere. While we were waiting for you.

DONOHUE. Who moved Mr. Wales' body? *(*C.*)*

CROSBY. *(C.)* I did.

DONOHUE. No one else touched him?

CROSBY. *(L.C.)* No one.

DONOHUE. What did you do, after you had carried him to the sofa?

CROSBY. I saw that he had been stabbed. I looked for the knife.

DONOHUE. Where?

CROSBY. On the floor, under the chairs, everywhere I could think of.

DONOHUE. No trace of it?

CROSBY. None.

DONOHUE. What did you do then?

CROSBY. Nothing. I waited for you.

DONOHUE. How long after you found that Mr. Wales was killed did you turn on the lights?

CROSBY. Why, I told you; we turned on the light before we found what had happened.

DONOHUE. Would it have been possible for the murderer to have hidden it about the room?

CROSBY. I doubt it very much.

DONOHUE. Why?

CROSBY. I don't think there would have been time. I don't see how anyone could have done it at all. It's all a mystery to me. I told you the circle was intact. You remember?

DONOHUE. *(There is a pause)* Yes, I remember. Then if the knife was hidden it's probably on the person of the man or woman who used it.

CROSBY. I think so, undoubtedly.

DONOHUE. Mike, phone over to the station house and have them send a matron over here. *(DUNN exits L. and closes the door after him)* Now about that light. There was just one lamp turned on, as I remember.

CROSBY. Someone turned on the rest of the lights, almost immediately.

DONOHUE. Could the knife have been hidden about the room, since that time?

CROSBY. It's extremely unlikely. We have all been here together. A thing of that sort would have been seen.

DONOHUE. Then I expect we'll find it without much trouble. (*There is a pause, as he looks slowly at each person individually in the room.* WILL *puts arm on* HELEN'S *shoulders as* DONOHUE *looks at him*) In the meantime, I think we'll let it remain where it is. (*Crosses down* R. *He turns with a gesture which takes them all in*) You see how inevitably the guilty person must be discovered. Don't you think it would be much simpler to confess? (*Pause*) No? Then I suppose we will have to continue. (*Crosses up* L., *gets chair—places it* L. *side of circle—then gets chair down* L., *places that in lower left-hand side of circle.* CROSBY *crosses to* C.) I'd like to visualize the scene a little more clearly. (TRENT *paces chair* L. *side of circle*) Let's form that circle again—— (*Turns two single chairs down* C., *around with backs to audience. Crosses and gets chair in front of table—places it lower right-hand side of circle.* MRS. CROSBY, ERSKINE, MRS. TRENT, TRENT *and* MISS STANDISH *rise, cross to* L. *of circle*) Of course, this time without Mr. Wales. (MISS EASTWOOD *rises, stands at* R. *end of settee. During these last few speeches of* DONOHUE, TRENT *and* CROSBY *have placed the remainder of chairs of the left-hand side in circle*) Won't you all sit as you were sitting at the seance?

(*By this time circle is formed completely with chairs. There is a general movement of those on the stage.* STANDISH *crosses* R. *to above table* R. *The minute this suggestion is made* ROSALIE *comes down, nearer to* DONOHUE *and looks at him anxiously.  Something in his suggestion greatly disturbs her.)*

CROSBY.  *(In upper L. side of circle)*  Will, you were there by the lamp, and Madame La Grange was next to you, and I was next to her——

DONOHUE.  Then how did they sit?  *(Down R.)*

CROSBY.  *(Next to* ROSALIE *L.C.)*  I'm trying to remember.  It's queer what a jumbled memory one has.  If anyone had asked me about it, I would have said I could have told how we were sitting with great accuracy.  But I can't somehow.

MISS ERSKINE.  I was next to you, Mr. Crosby. *(Upper L. side of circle.  She turns to* MRS. CROSBY, *who is standing over L.)*  Don't you remember, Mrs. Crosby, he said he'd always wanted to hold my hand, and we joked about it.  *(Sits in her original chair.)*

MRS. CROSBY.  *(L.—outside of circle)*  Yes.  I remember.

DONOHUE.  *(*HELEN *starts L.)*  That's all right, then.  Who came next?  *(Down R.  They all hesitate.)*

ROSALIE.  *(Eagerly)*  Inspector, I can place them all for you.

MASON.  *(Over end of table R.)*  But you said you didn't care how we sat.

*(*HELEN *R.C. in circle.)*

ROSALIE.  Nor did I, sorr.  But I was mighty careful to know where ye were sittin'.  Shall I show ye, Inspector?

DONOHUE.  *(After a pause)*  If you will be so kind.

ROSALIE.  *(*MISS STANDISH *sits in circle)*  The young lady was here.  Well, this gentleman was here.  *(Indicating* TRENT's *chair.)*

TRENT.  *(From L.—outside of circle)*  By George,

I couldn't have told you, but she's right. This is exactly where I was sitting. *(Sits in circle.)*

ROSALIE. *(Taking* HELEN *hastily by the shoulder and putting her in the next seat)* And this young lady was here. *(*HELEN *looks at her for a moment and then sinks back in her chair.* ROSALIE *points at* MASON*)* He came next.

MASON. *(Over* R.*)* No, you're wrong there. I —you're right. I remember perfectly I was next to Miss O'Neill. *(Crosses* L. *and sits* L. *side of circle)* I know just how her hand felt in the dark.

*(*WILL *looks at him quickly.* HELEN *turns and looks at him in wonder.)*

HELEN. *(Seated* L. *side in circle)* Well, really, Mr. Mason.

MASON. Oh, I don't mean it that way at all. I assure you I don't.

WILL. Then why did you say it? *(Seated* R.C.*)*

MASON. My dear fellow, I've apologized. You are misunderstanding me.

MRS. CROSBY. I think we're all pretty frazzled. *(*L. *outside of circle)* Inspector Donohue, must we go through all this again?

DONOHUE. I'm afraid so, Mrs. Crosby.

CROSBY. Then let's get it over as quickly as possible. *(Sits* C. *in circle.)*

DONOHUE. Mr. Crosby, you seem to forget that this is a police investigation, and must be conducted as I see fit. Who sat next to Mr. Mason?

ROSALIE. *(Pointing to* MISS EASTWOOD*)* This young lady.

MISS EASTWOOD. I was next to Mr. Mason, wasn't I, Phillip? *(Crossing inside of circle—to chair lower* L. *side of circle.)*

MASON. Yes.

DONOHUE. Now then, who occupied this seat?

MRS. TRENT. *(L.C. outside of circle)* Mr. Wales. I know because I sat *there,* and I was *next* to him. Shall I sit there now?

DONOHUE. If you will be so good.

*(MRS. TRENT crosses to R. and sits in circle.)*

STANDISH. I was next to Mrs. Trent. *(Upper end of table R. He sits.)*

MRS. CROSBY. And I was here between Mr. Standish and Billy. *(She sits. DONOHUE moves off a step down R. and stands looking at them as they sit. ROSALIE moves over and takes·her place in arm-chair.)*

DONOHUE. You are all sure that's where you were sitting?

MISS EASTWOOD. *(ROSALIE rises)* There's some mix-up here. I know. I wasn't next to Mr. Wales.

HELEN. *(Rises)* Of course you weren't. I don't see what I could have been thinking of, *I* sat where Miss Eastwood is.

MISS EASTWOOD. Yes, and I was next to Mr. Trent, between Phillip and Mr. Trent. I felt sure I was in the wrong seat. *(Rises.)*

DONOHUE. *(Quite casually)* Then if you ladies will exchange places. *(ROSALIE gives a little sigh of relief when she sees that DONOHUE attaches no importance to the substitution she has made. HELEN and MISS EASTWOOD change seats—HELEN crosses outside of circle)* Now, we're all right, aren't we? *(Slight buzz of conversation)* You are quite sure that you are all in the places you occupied during the seance?

CROSBY. Yes. I think so.

DONOHUE. *(He puts his hand on the empty chair)* We'll pretend that Mr. Wales is still sitting here. *(Slight movement from ALL)* Now, Mr. Crosby, I'll ask you to tell me what happened after the seance began.  But first I'll ask you this question : Was there any special arrangement about the seats?

ROSALIE.  *(Hurriedly—rises)*  There was not, sorr.  I towld them that they could sit anywhere they liked for all of me.  Young Mr. Crosby must have sat by the light on purpose.  And I'm sorry I made that mistake about the young ladies.  I don't know how I came to make a mistake like that.

DONOHUE.  Oh, well, if they couldn't remember where they sat, I don't see how I can expect you to be entirely accurate.  *(ROSALIE sits in armchair up c.)*  However, we're all right now.  Now, Mr. Crosby.  *(Down R.)*

CROSBY.  Well, after Madame La Grange had shown how she broke out of——

*(ALL look at DONOHUE.)*

DONOHUE.  We'll start with the seance.  I know how mediums break the circle and all that.  And you needn't describe how she went into that trance of hers.

MASON.  *(Seated in circle)*  Inspector, I don't think you're fair to this woman.  I think there's something pretty important that you haven't been told.

*(ALL look at MASON.)*

DONOHUE.  Then you'd better tell me now.

MASON.  In order that there should be no deception, we had Madame La Grange searched.

DONOHUE.  I see.

MASON.  And while she was out of the room——

DONOHUE.  Oh, she left the room?

*(ALL look at DONOHUE.)*

MASON. Yes, and all of the ladies went with her. Then someone suggested that we ask Madame La Grange about some special thing, and Mr. Wales said he was going to ask her to get in communication with Spencer Lee and see if we couldn't find out who killed him.

STANDISH. Most ridiculous thing——

MASON. As soon as she went into her trance, or whatever it was, Spencer Lee's spirit tried to talk to us.

DONOHUE. She began to give you messages from Spencer Lee without knowing that this was what you were trying to get?

MASON. *(In triumph)* Exactly. And there's no use in trying to tell me that there's nothing in spiritualism, because now I know better.

DONOHUE. Thank you very much, Mr. Mason. What you've told me is extremely important. I'm anxious to know what was said, because I'm a good deal interested in the Spencer Lee case myself.

*(MRS. TRENT turns and faces door, still sitting in her chair.)*

MASON. Then you think there's something in this spiritualism? I never did until to-day, but, by Jove, you know you can't expalin this any other way.

DONOHUE. Madame La Grange went into a trance. We'll grant that much, anyway. What happened then?

CROSBY. After a few minutes she began talking to us in the voice of a little child.

ROSALIE. That was Laughing Eyes, me spirit control.

DONOHUE. Just what did Laughing Eyes say?

CROSBY. It was all mixed up; none of it very clear. But she seemed to be trying to talk for someone to someone. She kept calling for Ned. Then suddenly she spoke deeply, in a man's voice.

DONOHUE. Did the man's message have any importance? I mean, did it seem to make sense?

CROSBY. It was perfectly coherent, at any rate. I can't give you the exact words, but——

MASON. *(Interrupting)* I can. He said, "Ned, I want Ned. Why in *hell* don't Ned answer me?"

DONOHUE. *(ALL seated in circle except DONOHUE, who is standing at lower end of table R.)* And did anyone answer?

CROSBY. Eventually Wales replied.

DONOHUE. I want you all to be extremely careful in what you tell me. I don't want any surmises. In the first place, did the message come for anyone but Mr. Wales?

CROSBY. There was at no time the mention of Wales' name. The calls were always for "Ned."

DONOHUE. I see. Did anyone else answer the calls?

STANDISH. *I* asked two or three questions, but no attention was paid to them.

DONOHUE. What did Mr. Wales say to all this?

CROSBY. I don't think Mr. Wales spoke at all until the message about saving his life came.

DONOHUE. And after that?

MISS EASTWOOD. There was a regular conversation between them.

CROSBY. *(MRS. TRENT puts handkerchief on lips)* Then there was some mention about some letters. I remember, too, that Mr. Wales said, "Are you trying to tell me who killed you?"

DONOHUE. What was the reply to that?

MRS. CROSBY. All we got were the words, "ASK—ask—ask."

CROSBY. And then I said, "Do you know who killed you?"

DONOHUE. Did you get an answer?

CROSBY. Not directly. The message was another cry for "Ned."

DONOHUE. What happened then?

CROSBY. Then Mr. Wales said, "Do you know who killed you?"

DONOHUE. *(Eagerly)* What answer did he get?

CROSBY. None. The medium began to moan and cry. Then Mr. Wales asked her again and again for the name. He kept crying, "Tell me who killed you, I want the name." He must have asked her two or three times. Then he cried out that he was hurt.

DONOHUE. And then?

CROSBY. That's all.

*(Enter* DUNN *from door* L.)

DUNN. The matron is here now, sir.

DONOHUE. Just a minute. Just one more question, Mr. Crosby. Did you get the impression that if Mr. Wales had not been killed, his question would have been answered?

CROSBY. If you grant that the seance was real, it would be impossible to arrive at any other conclusion.

DONOHUE. It was well established in your mind that Wales was the only person able to get a message?

CROSBY. Yes.

DONOHUE. It follows then that he was killed in order to prevent his question being answered.

CROSBY. That's the impression I got.

DONOHUE. This leads to the conclusion that whoever killed Wales knew who had killed Spencer Lee.

CROSBY. *(Still seated in circle)* I should think so.

DONOHUE. *(Front of table* R.) And it is not

difficult to surmise that the person who killed Wales was actuated by the strongest of all motives—self-protection. So in all human probability the murderer of Wales was also the murderer of Spencer Lee. You see, ladies and gentlemen, that by the use of a little patience we have come a long way in our investigation. *(There is a long pause)* I don't wish to put you all through the humiliation of a search. I should like to end this inquiry here and now. *(Breaks a step R. There is another pause)* No? Then we'll have to go on. *(Moves briskly—below table R.)* There is a police matron in the other room who will search the ladies of the party. Sergeant Dunn will perform a similar duty with the men. Mike, you will take them one at a time. It makes no difference to me in what order they go.

MASON. Well, I've got nothing to conceal. *(He rises and places chair up L., then to door L.)*

ROSALIE. Me neither. *(She rises and crosses down C.)*

DONOHUE. I'd rather you waited for a few minutes, Madame La Grange. *(ROSALIE looks at him sharply)* Any of the other ladies will do.

MRS. CROSBY. Suppose I set the others a good example? *(Rises.)*

DONOHUE. Thank you very much. *(He looks at the others, where they are still seated)* And thank you for the great help you've given me. You need not sit there any longer—(MRS. CROSBY comes down C., then crosses to door L.)—unless you wish.

*(MISS STANDISH crosses R. back of table R. MRS. CROSBY, MASON, and SERGEANT DUNN exit L. DUNN closes door on his exit. HELEN goes up C.—TRENT crosses one chair up L. of door L.C., then one chair R. of door L.C., right back of settee C. MISS ERSKINE crosses to back of table*

*R. MRS. TRENT seated R.C. WILL in front of settee C.)*

MISS EASTWOOD. *(Crossing to DONOHUE R.)* Inspector, I think you're perfectly wonderful.

DONOHUE. Oh, we haven't done very much yet, Miss Eastwood. Give the police a little time. *(He turns and crosses to L.C. L. with an abrupt change of tone)* Madame La Grange, there's a question I wish to ask you.

ROSALIE. *(Coming down to L.C.)* Anythin' at all, sor.

DONOHUE. *(L.C.)* When Mr. Wales asked you for the name, why didn't you answer him?

ROSALIE. I don't know, sor. I was in a trance. *(Down L.)*

DONOHUE. Then you didn't hear the question?

ROSALIE. How could I?

DONOHUE. I didn't ask you that. I want to know why you didn't answer him.

ROSALIE. I've already told you, I was in a trance. I didn't know what was going on.

DONOHUE. Why didn't you tell the name that you had agreed with Wales you would tell?

ROSALIE. *(L.C., astonished)* Agreed?

DONOHUE. You heard what I said. *(There is a pause)* Well, why didn't you carry out your part of the bargain? *(CROSBY crosses back of settee to C., front of settee)* Why didn't you give him the name as you'd planned?

ROSALIE. I don't know what ye mean.

DONOHUE. My words are perfectly plain. I asked you why you didn't carry out your part of the bargain?

ROSALIE. There wasn't any bargain!

DONOHUE. Your whole seance was a fake. *(Slight movement from OTHERS)* It was not only planned but rehearsed between you and Wales. He thought that a woman had killed his friend. He told you about it, and asked your help to discover the murderer.

ROSALIE. Sure, I don't know what ye're talking about at all.

DONOHUE. *(Ignoring her reply)* Every detail of this seance was planned. When he asked you the name you were to tell him the name of a woman.

*(MRS. TRENT crosses up* R. *and joins* TRENT *and* ERSKINE *at table* R.)

ROSALIE. So help me, Inspector, I never heard a word of this before.

DONOHUE. Not a word?

ROSALIE. So help me, not a word.

DONOHUE. *(*L.C. *Taking paper out of the inside pocket of his coat, and reading aloud)* "What do you want? Answer. Don't forget the swimming pool. Don't ever forget the swimming pool. Do you mean the time he went in after me when we were little boys? Spencer Lee says he can't rest." And so on and so on, down to—"Do you know who killed you?" *(He turns to the* OTHERS*)* The answer to that should have been "yes." What did she say?

CROSBY. *(In front of table* R.*)* She didn't answer that question.

DONOHUE. *(He looks at paper again.* L.C.*)* The next question is, "Can you tell the name?" And then she was to have told that woman's name. Just the first name. Mr. Crosby, what did she reply to that question?

CROSBY. She moaned and cried.

DONOHUE. What did she say after that?

CROSBY. Nothing. She moaned again and came out of so-called trance.

DONOHUE. Why didn't you do as you agreed?

ROSALIE. *(Down* L.C.L. *side of* DONOHUE *Stonily)* I don't know what you're talking about.

DONOHUE. The police know that some woman killed Spencer Lee. Something was taken from the inside pocket of his vest. We think it was a package of letters. This woman left traces. We have her fingerprints—many of them. Eventually we'll find her. For three or four weeks Mr. Wales has been working among the people who knew Lee. His theory was that this woman wanted to get back her letters—in fact, did get them back. He felt reasonably sure that he had found the woman. That one of you ladies here to-night is probably the woman we are hunting. He thought that he could play on her superstitious fears, and that when her name seemingly came from the spirit of the dead man she would confess. He told Madame La Grange the name, explained to her just what he wanted, and together he and I worked out the exact wording of the messages that were supposed to come from Spencer Lee's spirit. *(He turns suddenly to* ROSALIE, *who is down* L.C.*)* You agreed to all this; why didn't you speak the name?

ROSALIE. I don't know anything about it  He— he must have forgotten to tell it to me.

DONOHUE. Oh, no, he didn't.

*(*EASTWOOD *down in front of table* R.*)*

ROSALIE. *(With great decision)* There was no name. He didn't tell me any name.

DONOHUE. My good woman, you mustn't take me for a fool. You agreed to use a certain name; you came here for that purpose, and then after you got here something happened to make you change your plans. Something unexpected happened. *(He stops for a moment—turns to* MISS EASTWOOD*)* Miss Eastwood, what did you say was your first name?

MISS EASTWOOD. Mary.

DONOHUE. *(To* MISS ERSKINE*)* And yours?

MISS ERSKINE. *(Back of table* R.*)* Elizabeth.

DONOHUE. Yours?

MISS STANDISH. Grace.

DONOHUE. Mr. Crosby, your wife's given name is——

CROSBY. Alicia.

DONOHUE. Mrs. Trent?

MRS. TRENT. *(*R.C.*)* Helen.

DONOHUE. Miss O'Neill?

HELEN. *(Up* C.*)* Helen. *(There is a long pause.)*

DONOHUE. *(*L.C. WILL *comes to* HELEN C.*)* Helen, I see. So there are two Helens. Two Helens. *(He stands looking first at one and then at the other of the two women)* Mr. Crosby, when Madame La Grange first came to-night did she show any surprise at seeing any of the people here?

CROSBY. *(*R.C.*)* Not that I noticed.

MISS EASTWOOD. *(Below table* R.*)* Oh, yes, she did. Miss O'Neill wasn't in the room when she arrived. Later when she came in the old woman seemed upset. She said something to her that none of us could hear. Then I remember she argued with Mr. Wales and said she didn't feel like having a seance.

DONOHUE. Now we're getting it. *(*WILL *stands* R. *of* MISS O'NEILL *up* C.*)* Everything was going along smoothly, until Miss O'Neill came in. The extra Helen. *(He turns to* CROSBY*)* Mr. Crosby, your daughter was in the room when Madame La Grange came in?

CROSBY. Yes.

DONOHUE. You noticed nothing unusual in this woman's manner?

CROSBY. I'd never seen her before.

DONOHUE. I mean she did nothing to attract your

attention; the fact that Helen Trent was in the room made no impression on her?

CROSBY. Seemingly not.

DONOHUE. Then Helen O'Neill came in. *(Goes up to* HELEN *c., then crosses to* ROSALIE L. *He turns sharply to* ROSALIE *down* L.*)* Rosalie La Grange, what's that girl to you?

ROSALIE. Nothin' at all.

DONOHUE. *(c.)* Nothing at all! Then why did you try to deceive me as to where she sat? Why did you place her so that I would not know she was sitting next to Mr. Wales when he was stabbed?

ROSALIE. It was just a mistake. I didn't go for to do it.

DONOHUE. I'm afraid that won't do. It's perfectly apparent that the name you were to speak was—Helen. *(He turns to* ROSALIE L.*)* What's the use of lying to me? You've tried your best to shield this girl. I want to know why.

ROSALIE. There's no reason. I never saw the young lady before in all my life.

DONOHUE. What's that girl to you?

ROSALIE. Nothin', nothin' at all——

DONOHUE. *(Starts to* ROSALIE*)* Damn you, you old harridan, you come across——

MISS O'NEILL *(Springing forward from up* R.C. *down to* L., *throwing* DONOHUE *up stage)* Let my mother alone, let my mother alone! *(Then she goes to* ROSALIE, *puts arms around her.—Pause.—*ROSALIE *weeps.)*

DONOHUE. *(Very quietly)* I thought perhaps I'd get it that way.

HELEN O'NEILL. *(Getting* L. *side of* ROSALIE*)* There, there, dear, it's all right, it's all right.

DONOHUE. *(With a grim smile, coming down* C.*)* Of course, it's all right! We've got the finger prints and——

WILL. *(Interrupting him—crosses down to* C.*)*

If you think for one minute I'm going to let you——

CROSBY. My son, wait—*(Grabbing him and pinning down his arms to sides* c.*)*—think what——

WILL. Think nothing. *(He shakes himself free and goes to* DONOHUE L.C.*)* That's the girl I love, and I'll be *damned* if I let you take her finger prints.

DONOHUE. Young man, don't be a fool. I'm sorry, but it's too clear.

ROSALIE. *(Breaking away from her daughter to* DONOHUE C. *of* L.C.*)* Clear! Glory be to God, how can it be clear? Inspector, you're never goin' to accuse me little girl of a thing like that?

DONOHUE. *(*C.*)* She was next to him; she had only to free one hand, and strike and then take his hand again!

ROSALIE. There was something else she had to do before she could ever do that. She had to have murder in her heart.

DONOHUE. *(*C.*)* Well?

ROSALIE. *(Turns suddenly, seizes her daughter, who is* L. *of* DONOHUE, *by the hand, turns her to him.—*ROSALIE *stays between* DONOHUE *and* HELEN*)* Look at her. Look in the eyes of her, at the face of her. Is there murder there? Man, man, haven't ye got eyes in yer head?

*(*DUNN *enters from* L.*)*

DUNN. It's not on either of them.

DONOHUE. I know where it is. Tell the matron she'll find the knife on this girl.

ROSALIE. *(To* DONOHUE C.*)* Inspector, for Gawd's sake, don't do it! I'll tell you anything I know, only keep your hands off me little girl. I did come here like you say, and whin I seen me own child I lost me head. I'm a poor old woman that ain't got any sense. I tried to save her and I only made matters worse. You've looked at her, the poor young thing that wouldn't harm a fly, and you think she could do a thing like that?

DONOHUE.    Yes.

ROSALIE.    *(Still crying bitterly)*  Thin Tim Donohue, you're a damn fool, and God helpin' me, I'll prove ut.

## CURTAIN

# ACT III

SCENE: *The eight small chairs that were brought on in the First Act, are taken off stage. The big armchair that* ROSALIE *sat in has been taken up the left corner of set. Table has been moved up and on stage about a foot. The knife that is to fall on given cue has been placed in slot in ceiling. The window blind is pulled down, the curtains on window are opened. Armchair back of table right. Chair below table right. Chair above table right. Settee has been moved down stage centre about a foot. Shelf back of settee has been fixed for* WALES *to lie on. Console table back in its original position, right end of settee centre. Chairs with upholstered seat put back to left side of fireplace. Line hung off stage back of fireplace for policeman's entrance. Bright amber lights in entrance down left. Lamps with blue mediums at window LIT. Spot outside of window right ready for cue. Lights on set out. Door down left, which is open.*

*Be sure to clear table* R.C. *for knife.*

DISCOVERED: ROSALIE *by table over right.*

ROSALIE. Father in Heaven, help me. Me Nelly's in trouble, terrible trouble, and there ain't any wan to help her but me. She's a good girl—you know all things, you know she's a good girl. Show me the way. Sure, I been a fakir all my life. I've tricked 'em and fooled 'em, but honest, I never

75

meant to harm a soul, I never knowingly done harm to any wan. And there is a power. It's come to me before, a way of knowin', that I couldn't understand. I felt it, and I showed it. Oh, God, give it to me again. Do this for my little girl, for the sake of your Son. Amen.

*(Turns and goes up stage to the window at R. She pulls up the shade and raises the window. The light comes up from the street lamp, throwing out her figure in strong silhouette, and showing a square patch of light on the ceiling. In the center of this patch, sticking point up in the heavy wooden paneling, can be seen the knife. ROSALIE stands for a few moments looking out at the night. DONOHUE enters down L. As he does so, he turns on the lights from the switch below the door down L. Lights in room on. Spot outside of window—OUT.)*

DONOHUE. *(Crosses to L.C.)* Who turned off the lights?

ROSALIE. *(At window R.)* I did, sor.

DONOHUE. Why?

ROSALIE. I was prayin'. *(Coming to above table R.)*

DONOHUE. Praying? What for?

ROSALIE. Guidance.

DONOHUE. *(With a laugh)* I hope you get it.

ROSALIE. *(With conviction)* I will, sor, I will. *(She starts toward the door L.)* I'll be joinin' the others now.

DONOHUE. I think you'd better wait. *(Calls off L.)* Mike. *(ROSALIE C.)*

*(DUNN enters from L.)*

DUNN. Yes, Inspector?

DONOHUE.  Did Madame La Grange see you as she came in here?

DUNN.  *(Down* L.)  No, sir.  I followed your instructions and kept out of sight.

DONOHUE.  How long has she been here?  *(*L.C.*)*

DUNN.  About ten minutes.

DONOHUE.  Time enough for her to find what we couldn't.

DUNN.  I'll bet she's got it.

DONOHUE.  Take her to Mrs. MacPherson.  She's not to go near anyone or speak to anyone.  Tell Mrs. Mac to search her.  *(He turns to* ROSALIE, *who is* C.*)*  Unless, of course, you want to give up that knife now.

ROSALIE.  I've got no knife, and I've been searched once.

DONOHUE.  *(*L.C.*)*  Exactly, and then you were allowed to come back into this room.  We're rather anxious to see what you've found while you were in here.  Well?

ROSALIE.  I found nothing that ud be any good to you.

DONOHUE.  I'm the best judge of that.  What was it you found?

ROSALIE.  A sort of comfort, sor.  A feelin' that the innocent would come to no harm.

DONOHUE.  *(Dryly)*  Take her to Mrs. Mac-Pherson.  Come back as soon as you turn her over to the matron.

DUNN.  Yes, Inspector.  Come on—come on, you.

ROSALIE.  *(Crossing* L.*)*  I'm coming!

*(They exit.  He stands looking after them for count of five when* DUNN *re-enters and says.)*

DUNN.  *(Above door* L.*)*  Mrs. Mac's got her.

DONOHUE.  *(To* DUNN*)*  She turned out that

light. I wonder why? What did she want in the dark?

*(He goes over toward the light switch at L. and puts out his hand. He stops suddenly as his attention is attracted by a policeman coming feet foremost down the chimney. DONOHUE gives a little start and then comes L.C. The Policeman jumps down all the way in fireplace, and comes into the room to console table L. end of settee. His uniform is covered with soot, and so are his face and hands. DUNN goes down L. below door.)*

DUNN. I sent him to see if they'd hidden that knife up there?

DONOHUE. Good. *(To POLICEMAN)* Find anything?

POLICEMAN. Nothing but dirt. Who pays for this uniform?

DONOHUE. You don't, anyway. Could you hear anything while you were up there?

POLICEMAN. Not a thing.

DONOHUE. You are sure?

POLICEMAN. Certain.

DONOHUE. Go take a bath.

POLICEMAN. 'Tain't Saturday. *(He exits at L. DONOHUE crosses R. Pause.)*

DUNN. *(Down L. After a pause)* Don't it beat *hell?*

DONOHUE. Why?

DUNN. That knife couldn't have flew away.

DONOHUE. *(Coming C.)* We'll find it eventually. It's in this room somewhere.

DUNN. No, sir, it ain't.

DONOHUE. Where have you looked?

DUNN. Everywhere.

DONOHUE. Not hidden in the furniture?

Dunn. I'll gamble it ain't. Took up all the rugs, shook 'em. Dug through the upholstery in the furniture, looked back of mat on the wall. It's not in the bric-a-brac or whatever these swells call their jugs.

(Donohue *crosses to table* r.)

Donohue. (r.c.) Unless we find it on the old woman, it's still in this room.

Dunn. I suppose you noticed that she opened the window?

Donohue. (*Upper end of table* r.) Yes, I noticed that. Mike, you've the makings of a great detective.

Dunn. I'm a darned good detective now.

(Donohue *goes to window at* r. *and calls out.*)

Donohue. Say, Doolan! See anything?

Doolan. (*Outside window* r.) An old woman put up the window just now. She stood there a while looking up in the air—(*Pause*)—watching the stars, I guess.

Donohue. Have anything in her hand?

Doolan. No, sir. The light from this lamp was shinin' right on her. I could see everything.

Donohue. Throw anything out of the window?

Doolan. No, Inspector.

Donohue. All right. You're to arrest anyone leaving the house.

Doolan. I gotcha.

(Donohue *comes below table* r.; *turns to* Dunn. *Crosses to* l.c.)

Donohue. We'll find the knife eventually. We've got to. Get me Mr. Crosby and the O'Neill girl—that's the order I want to see them in here.

*(DUNN exits L. DONOHUE crosses up R. end of set-*
*tee to chest up R., starts to cross L. below settee.*
*—CROSBY closes door, enters down L.—DONO-*
*HUE comes down to C.—R. end of settee.)*

CROSBY. *(To L.C.)* Your man told me to come here.

DONOHUE. Yes. Sorry to have to give orders in your house. If you don't like it I can take every-one down to Police Headquarters. You know what will happen—what the newspapers will do if I take all these ladies and gentlemen down town. In the end this way will be the best for you and your friends. Well, how about it?

CROSBY. *(L.C.)* Thank you. I think you'd bet-ter regard this house as your own for the present.

DONOHUE. *(C.)* All right. If you don't mind I'll use this room as a headquarters for the present.

CROSBY. I have already told you to use this house as your own.

DONOHUE. Thank you. Good evening.

CROSBY. *(With a laugh)* I'm dismissed?

DONOHUE. You're dismissed. *(CROSBY walks toward door L.)* Why did Wales object to the en-gagement of your son and Helen O'Neill?

CROSBY. *(Turns to DONOHUE)* Who told you that? *(R. a few steps.)*

DONOHUE. It doesn't matter. I know that he did. Why?

CROSBY. I can't talk about it. *(Turns front.)*

DONOHUE. *(C.)* All right. You're the best judge of that. Only I'm attaching a great deal of importance to this fact. If I'm unduly emphasizing its value, don't you think you'd better set me straight about it?

CROSBY. What possible bearing can it have on——

DONOHUE. Motive, my dear sir, motive.

CROSBY. Come now—you can't think that this girl killed Wales because she heard him ask us to wait before we sanctioned her engagement to my son.

DONOHUE. She did hear Mr. Wales make that objection? That's just what I wanted to know.

CROSBY. (L.) I think I'd better send for my lawyer.

DONOHUE. (C.) Well, you can do as you like about that. Frankly, I don't understand your attitude at all. I can appreciate your desire to spare your son all the unhappiness that you can. But if this young woman killed Wales and Lee, the sooner we find it out the better for you and your family.

CROSBY. Oddly enough, I was thinking only of Miss O'Neill at the moment.

DONOHUE. You'd better think of yourself and your family first. *(Crosses R. a few steps.)*

                                    *READY KNOCK*

CROSBY. That's for me to decide, sir. I certainly am not going to allow that child to be bullied and badgered in the usual police fashion. *(Crosses R. a step.)*

DONOHUE. You're going to do as you are told, sir. If you warn that girl, if you caution her in any way, I'll drag everyone of you down town. You and your wife and your son and the girl and all your friends. Be reasonable, Mr. Crosby. If the girl is innocent, telling me the truth won't hurt her. If she's guilty, and I think she is, by God, I'm going to drag the truth out of her and her mother. *(Knock on the door down L.)* Come in.

HELEN. *(Enters L.)* You wanted me?

DONOHUE. Yes, come in. Sit down, please. *(In-*

*dicating table below* R.—HELEN *sits.*—CROSBY
*starts* R.)

CROSBY. Helen.

DONOHUE. What you are planning to do, Mr.
Crosby, will only make matters worse, I promise you
that. *(After a moment's pause* CROSBY *exits at* L.
*and leaves door open.* DONOHUE *turns, closes door
and turns sharply to* HELEN—*crosses to table* R.)
Now then, young woman, let's hear what you've got
to say.

HELEN. Nothing.

DONOHUE. (C.) Nothing. I don't suppose it's
necessary for me to tell you that you're under grave
suspicion.

HELEN. No, I realize that.

DONOHUE. Now the best way to help yourself
if you're innocent is to be quite frank with me.
*(She simply looks at him, but does not speak)* Well?

HELEN. I've already told you that there is nothing that I can say.

DONOHUE. Someone has advised you not to answer me. Who was it? *(There is a pause)* You'd
better tell me. *(Crosses* R.C.)

HELEN. I am not going to answer any of your
questions.

DONOHUE. I told you that if you were innocent,
nothing that you could say would hurt you. If
you're guilty—well, that's a different matter.

HELEN. You know that I didn't do it.

DONOHUE. *(In front of table* R.) Well, there
you are. Why not answer my questions, then?
The sooner we find out who is guilty the sooner
you'll be freed from suspicion. You see that, don't
you?

HELEN. Yes.

DONOHUE. *(Brings chair and sits in front of
table* R.) Now we're getting along. How well did
you know Spencer Lee? *(*HELEN *does not answer*

*him—looking front)* You'd better make up your mind to talk. Do you hear? *(HELEN does not speak. Losing his temper)* Why, you little fool, do you think you can fight me? *(He turns sharply to face her, turning his back on the door at L.)* You were the last person to see Spencer Lee alive. Yes, and you saw him dead, too. You heard Wales threaten to tell these fine people what he knew about you; you knew he'd prevent your marriage to this young millionaire, and then—*(ROSALIE enters quietly from L. and stands for a moment watching them)*—when your chance came in the dark, you killed him. Now then, you come across with the truth.

ROSALIE. She'll come across with nothin'. *(Crosses R. to table. DONOHUE rises and stands by table R.C. HELEN rises)* Ye said she was the wan that did ut and ye'd find the knife on her. Well, ye didn't, did ye? Ye think she's the wan that killed Spencer Lee?

DONOHUE. Yes.

ROSALIE. Well, she ain't. Ye say ye got the finger prints of the girl that was in his rooms—now take Nelly's, then. Take hers and put 'em alongside of the others, bad cess to you, and then ye'll see. I dare ye do that.

HELEN. *(With a cry)* Mother! *(She stops suddenly.)*

DONOHUE. What were you going to say?

HELEN. Nothing. *(She creeps over to R. side of her mother. ROSALIE puts her arms about the girl.)*

. *(DUNN enters with box and envelope.)*

DONOHUE. That's very wise of you.

DUNN. Got it, Inspector. *(Crosses to C.)*

DONOHUE. *(Down R.)* Do they compare?

DUNN. To a T.

*(ROSALIE C., HELEN down R. DONOHUE in front of table between HELEN and ROSALIE.)*

DONOHUE. All right. Let me have 'em. Now ask Mr. Crosby and his son to come here at once. *(DUNN turns and exits at L. DONOHUE up C., crosses to back of table R.)* I already have your daughter's fingerprints, Madame La Grange.

ROSALIE. Have ye, now? It's smart ye are.

*(HELEN crosses to ROSALIE R.C. ROSALIE swings HELEN L. of her. When DONOHUE opens box back of table, CROSBY and WILL enter from L., accompanied by DUNN.)*

DONOHUE. That's all, Mike. *(DUNN exits at L., closes door down L. CROSBY L. of HELEN. WILL L. of CROSBY)* Mr. Crosby, I told you that I'd settle this case in a few minutes. The end has come sooner than I thought. I am now ready to make an arrest. I have sent for you and your son because—— *(He suddenly turns toward HELEN)* This is the woman we have been hunting.

ROSALIE. That's a lie! *(R. end of settee—WILL to HELEN.)*

DONOHUE. *(Picking up cup and holding it out toward them)* Here is the cup—*(CROSBY crosses down R. to below table—moves chair over R.)*— which we took from Spencer Lee's rooms. These are the fingerprints of the woman who used it. *(Ignoring CROSBY for the moment)* Here is the saucer that she used. More fingerprints. A few minutes ago I sent this young woman a note. The man who gave it to her wore gloves, so did I when I addressed the envelope. Hers are the only naked hands that have touched it. *(He picks up the envelope gingerly by one corner, and holds it outward to them)* They are unquestionably Helen O'Neill's fingerprints. *(HELEN in WILL'S arms. DONOHUE puts down the envelope. Then he picks up the cup and points to the fingermarks on it)* And so, Mr. Crosby, are these. There can be no doubt about it. There is never any doubt about this method of identification. In twenty years there has never been one mistake. We now have what we've been hunting for. The woman who went to Spencer Lee's rooms. *(DONOHUE steps back with a little gesture of triumph. CROSBY stands staring at the girl. ROSALIE comes to R. of HELEN, turns to her.)*

ROSALIE. *(C.)* Look at me, me dear. Look at your old mother. *(She takes HELEN'S face in her hands and looks at her closely. Then, with a little cry of contentment, stands R. of HELEN. ROSALIE and HELEN back up to settee)* Now, me dear, ye mustn't be frightened. Look up, child. Why don't ye say somethin'?

HELEN. I can't. *(Sits on settee.)*

*(DONOHUE gives a short laugh.)*

DONOHUE. What can she say?

WILL. *(Going to her)* Dear, tell him it's a lie.

CROSBY. *(Crosses to HELEN, at settee)* Wait. Let me talk to her. *(CROSBY comes over to HELEN and sits beside her on the sofa, R. side. WILL at settee L. end)* My dear, you understand that none of us believe—what the Inspector wants us to believe. We know that you have never done anything —that you are no more guilty of this atrocious crime than I am. We all want to help you. You understand that, don't you?

HELEN. Yes.

WILL. I won't have this.

CROSBY. I'm afraid you must, son. *(He turns again to HELEN)* We want to help you, so, my dear, you must be perfectly frank with us. Inspector Donohue says he can prove that you went to that man's rooms.  Is that true?

HELEN.  *(Slowly and reluctantly)*  Yes.

*(*DONOHUE *gives short laugh.  Sits back of table* R.)

ROSALIE.  An' what if she did?—She had a good errant.—What did ye go for, darlin'?

HELEN.  I can't tell you.

WILL.  Dear, you must tell us.  *(She looks at him suddenly.  He comes over and kneels beside her and talks to her as if to a little child)*  My dear, it isn't that we don't trust you.  Surely you know how we all love you.  But we must know the truth—*(Strong)*—because we have to show *him* how wrong he is.

DONOHUE.  *(Seated back of table* R.)  Yes, and I'm waiting to be shown.

WILL.  *(Kneeling* L. *of* HELEN *by settee)*  Why did you go to Spencer Lee?

HELEN.  *(Sitting on settee)*  You mustn't ask me that.  I can't tell you.

CROSBY.  *(Still on settee)*  But if you don't tell us, how can we help you?

HELEN.  I didn't do anything.  I didn't do anything.

CROSBY.  We know that, my child.  But why did you go?  *(*HELEN *does not answer)*  Did you know Spencer Lee?

WILL.  Of course she didn't.

DONOHUE.  *(Seated back of table* R.)  Why don't she speak for herself?

WILL.  Because I'll speak for her.

CROSBY.  Can't you answer even that question?

*(*HELEN *shakes her head and makes a despairing gesture.)*

WILL. But, dear, don't you see what they'll think? Helen, you must tell me.

HELEN. Could I speak to mother, alone? *(Rises.)*

DONOHUE. You cannot.

*(CROSBY and WILL rise, cross to C. CROSBY crosses to L. end of settee.)*

ROSALIE. *(R. end of settee)* Where's the harm in that? Sure, a child's the right to talk to her own mother any time she wants.

DONOHUE. Anything you wish to say, you can say in front of me.

ROSALIE. *(Coming to HELEN C.)* Sure, darlin', ye needn't mind the nice Inspector. Don't I well know that there was never anything in your mind that ye couldn't say before all the world? *(There is a pause)* Tell yer old mother, me dear.

*(CROSBY C. WILL standing below him C.)*

HELEN. *(Beginning to cry)* I can't. I can't.

ROSALIE. *(C.)* Stop, there's been cryin' enough. I lost me head through that and me fears. Stop cryin' or I'll give ye what for. *(She, too, begins to cry and takes her daughter in her arms again)* There, there, me dear. Sure, yer old mother ain't going to let anyone hurt ye. Not anyone at all. *(They cry together for a moment and then ROSALIE gets her self-control back. She blows her nose vigorously)* We'll both be the better for that. Now then, tell me.

HELEN. Mother, I can't.

ROSALIE. *(R.C.)* Who did ye promise ye wouldn't?

HELEN. *(Surprised)* Why, how did you——

ROSALIE. She's shieldin' someone.

HELEN.   No. No.

ROSALIE.   And that's the first lie ye ever told, and I know it.  I want to know who ye're shieldin'? *(HELEN does not answer.  ROSALIE suddenly turns to WILL)*  Is she your girl?

WILL.   Yes. *(L.C.)*

ROSALIE.   Then make her tell.

WILL.   *(To HELEN C.)*  Nell, dear, you must——

HELEN.   Billy, I can't.

CROSBY.   *(Drops down L. of group)*  My dear, even if you're protecting someone else, I think you ought to tell us.

HELEN.   *(With a sudden outburst)*  Why are you all against me?  Why are you all trying to make me break my—— *(To R. end of settee.  WILL comes to her.  CROSBY L.C.)*

ROSALIE.   *(Interrupting HELEN, coming to R.C.)*  Break yer word, is ut?  Ye should not.  Sure, there never was an O'Neill in the world that was an informer.  Ye needn't tell.  Sure, I know it meself now.  'Tis blind I've been. *(She turns suddenly on the INSPECTOR—to down table R. above him)*  Ye're the one that found out there was two Helens.  The extra Helen, says you.  Well, send for the other Helen and ask her.

HELEN.   Mother, stop!

ROSALIE.   Stop, is ut?  Sure, I will not.

CROSBY.   *(C.)*  Wait, please.  Is it my daughter you're protecting? *(HELEN does not answer)*  Because if it is—much as we love her, my dear, we can't accept that sacrifice from you.  I'm her father, and you must tell me the truth.  Did my daughter send you? *(There is a long pause)*  Did you go for my daughter?

HELEN.   *(Slowly)*  Yes.

ROSALIE.   I knew ut. *(Above table R.)*

CROSBY.   My daughter sent you.  What for?

HELEN.   *(R.C.)*  Some letters.

WILL. *(In front of settee* C.*)* Why didn't she go herself?

HELEN. She was afraid.

DONOHUE. *(Still seated back of table* R.*)* Well, go on. (HELEN *does not speak.)*

WILL. (R.C.) Tell him, dear, it's all right.

HELEN. I don't know what to say.

DONOHUE. Why not tell the truth? *(Rises to chair below table* R.*)*

ROSALIE. Tell the Inspector what happened, dearie. *(Putting* HELEN *in chair front of table* R.*)*

HELEN. Nothing happened. That's the funny part of it. The minute Mr. Lee understood that I knew about the letters, everything was changed. I said that unless he gave them to me I'd tell Mr. Crosby about them. He seemed terribly upset. He said he hadn't meant to frighten Helen. That he loved her, and was desperate. I thought it was a funny kind of love, but I didn't tell him that. Then he gave me the letters.

DONOHUE. Was this before or after you had tea with him?

HELEN. Before.

DONOHUE. Go on. He gave you the letters.

HELEN. *(Seated in front of table* R.*)* Yes. And he seemed terribly unhappy. He begged me to stay and talk to him for a few minutes, and I did. He asked me to have some tea with him, and I did that, too.

DONOHUE. How charming! What did you do after tea?

*(*ROSALIE *back of chair, front of table.)*

HELEN. I came home and gave Helen her letters.

DONOHUE. And that's all?

HELEN. That's all. *(Saucy.)*

DONOHUE. Why did you do this?

HELEN. *(Seated front of table* R.*)* She's Billy's sister.

DONOHUE. My compliments, young woman. That was beautifully done. And she looks so innocent, too.

WILL. You don't believe—— *(*C.*)*

DONOHUE. Not a word of it. Not one word. *(Rises.)*

ROSALIE. And why not?

DONOHUE. That I *don't* is sufficient. Her story is preposterous. Your daughter's——

WILL. It's the truth.

DONOHUE. Do you expect me to believe for a minute that a man like Lee would threaten your daughter, and then when a total stranger comes to him and asks for the letters, give them up without a word? Why, no jury in the world would believe your story.

WILL. Jury? You're not going to arrest her?

DONOHUE. She is arrested.

ROSALIE. Ye got no proof.

DONOHUE. *(Below table* R.*)* All the proof that I need. If she was innocent, why didn't she tell me all this when I first questioned her? Why did she wait until she knew that I had proof—that she had been in Spencer Lee's rooms?

WILL. She was protecting my sister.

DONOHUE. Women don't hang together like that.

ROSALIE. *(Upper end of table* R.*)* Sure they do. The poor creatures.

DONOHUE. *(Down* R.*)* They do not. I know them. *(He turns to* WILL*)* She wasn't protecting your sister. She was protecting herself. She went for the letters, of course; and they had tea before she asked for them, not afterwards.

CROSBY. *(*R.C. *to* L. *of* WILL*)* How do you know that?

DONOHUE. She couldn't take tea with a man she's just killed.

WILL. Why, *damn* you—— *(Starts R.)*

CROSBY. *(Grabbing WILL by shoulders)* Billy!

WILL. *(Breaks up stage a few steps, then down stage again)* I'm sorry. I didn't mean to lose my temper. I suppose we've got to take this thing calmly. Inspector, you honestly believe that Nelly killed this man?

DONOHUE. Yes.

WILL. Why should she?

DONOHUE. She was engaged to you—he had compromising letters she had written to him—he was threatening her with exposure—she went to get her letters. They had tea together—she's admitted that, after we proved it, and then when he wouldn't give up her letters, she killed him. So much for the first murder. *(Turns away)* Now for the second: she was sitting next to Wales; he had already threatened her with exposure; in another minute, the medium would have told her name as that of the person who had been at Spencer Lee's rooms. She pulled her hand away from his, struck, and took his hand again. *(There is a pause)* Young man, you'll have a hard time tearing apart that chain of evidence.

ROSALIE. Barrin' the fact that she niver wrote the man a letter in her loife, 'tis a grand case ye got.

WILL. *(Down C. a step. CROSBY goes above WILL C.)* Of course. Dad, we've lost our brains. She didn't go for her own letters. *(WILL turns to the INSPECTOR)* You were talking of juries. Do you think any jury will believe that a young girl would kill a man to get back another woman's letters for her? *(He starts toward door L.)*

CROSBY. Where are you going?

WILL. To get my sister.

DONOHUE. Wait. *(WILL stops)* I'll send for Mrs. Trent.

WILL. *(Crosses L.C.)* But I want to ask her——

DONOHUE. *(Interrupts him)* I'll ask my own questions. If you want to help this investigation, you might call Sergeant Dunn for me.

*(WILL opens door at L.)*

WILL. *(Crosses to C.)* Sergeant Dunn, the Inspector wants you. *(He turns back to the girl and DUNN enters L.)*

DONOHUE. Ask Mrs. Trent to come here. *(DUNN exits at L. ROSALIE R. end of settee. HELEN in chair in front of table R. WILL C. CROSBY walks up L., then back to L.C. DONOHUE below the table, looking at them with a grim smile. After a pause of ten counts, MRS. TRENT and TRENT enter from L., followed by DUNN, who stands below the door)* I sent for Mrs. Trent.

TRENT. I know that. What do you want to see her about? *(L.C.)*

DONOHUE. Mrs. Trent, did you ask this girl to go to Spencer Lee's rooms to get letters you had written to him?

TRENT. *(L. of MRS. TRENT)* Did she what?

DONOHUE. Did you, Mrs. Trent?

MRS. TRENT. *(L.C.)* Certainly not.

HELEN. Why—— *(Rises from chair in front of table R.)*

DONOHUE. *(Sternly)* Keep still, you. *(To MRS. TRENT)* Are you sure?

TRENT. *(L. of MRS. TRENT)* Of course she's sure.

DONOHUE. Mr. Trent, you must stop these interruptions. *(To MRS. TRENT)* Will you please answer my question?

MRS. TRENT. I never wrote a letter to Spencer

**Lee** in my life. *(She suddenly turns to* HELEN*)* How dare you say I sent you there?

HELEN. You did! You did! *(Front of table.)*

MRS. TRENT. *(Down* L.C.*)* I don't know what she's told you, Inspector, but——

DONOHUE. Never mind what she told me. I want to be very sure of this. You did not ask this girl to go to Spencer Lee's rooms?

MRS. TRENT. No.

DONOHUE. *(Down* R.*)* He had no letters of yours?

MRS. TRENT. *(*L.C.*)* No.

DONOHUE. Do you know whether this girl had written to him?

MRS. TRENT. I don't know anything about it.

WILL. *(Coming* L. *of* MRS. TRENT. CROSBY *to* C.*)* But Nell didn't know Lee, and Helen, you did.

DONOHUE. *(Still down* R.*)* How about that, Mrs. Trent?

MRS. TRENT. I hadn't seen Mr. Lee in two or three years. He used to come here a good deal. He wanted to marry me, but I didn't like him. And I certainly never wrote him letters of any sort. That is all I can tell you.

DONOHUE. Thank you very much. That is all that I want to know.

WILL. *(Turning on his sister)* You're lying to save yourself. You've got to tell the truth.

TRENT. She is telling you the truth.

WILL. She's not.

CROSBY. *(After a pause, putting his hand on his son's shoulder)* I'm sorry, Billy.

*(*WILL *goes up to settee* C., *sits.* CROSBY *looks coldly at* HELEN *and turns to his daughter.)*

MRS. TRENT. Father, you know that——

CROSBY. Yes, dear—I know. Inspector, do you want us any more?

DONOHUE. Not any more, thank you——

CROSBY. Come then, children—— *(He exits with* MR. *and* MRS. TRENT *down* L. HELEN *still in front of table* R.*)*

DONOHUE. *(As the door closes. Crosses* L. *to* L.C.*)* Mike, take her down town.

ROSALIE. *(C.)* I wouldn't if I was you. Inspector, I know who done it. *(*WILL *rises.)*

DONOHUE. *(Turning to* ROSALIE C.*)* You know —who was it?

ROSALIE. I can't tell you yet. *(*DONOHUE *laughs.* WILL R.C. *Crosses to* HELEN*)* But I will. I will!

DONOHUE. Tellin's not enough. There's just one thing that will convince me that she didn't kill Spencer Lee.

WILL. *(Down* R.*)* What, Inspector, what?

DONOHUE. The confession of the one who did. *(He turns to* ROSALIE*)* Bring me that and I'll set your daughter free.

ROSALIE. *(C.)* Inspector, give me a chance. Don't arrest me little girl. Give me time. I know who done it and I'll get ye what ye want.

DONOHUE. *(L.C.)* Nonsense.

ROSALIE. *(Crosses* L. *to* INSPECTOR*)* Give me an hour, sor, keep them all here an hour more.

*(*WILL *crosses down* R. *to* HELEN.*)*

DONOHUE. No.

WILL. *(*WILL *and* HELEN *in front of table* R.*)* Give her a chance. We're all here—no one will get away. What difference will a few minutes make?

*(There is a pause.* DONOHUE *takes out his watch and looks at it.)*

DONOHUE.   I'll give her ten minutes, Mike.   Tell
Doolan again to arrest anyone trying to leave the
house and get on the front door yourself and stay
there until I tell you.   *(DUNN turns and exits at L.)*
You've got just ten minutes.   *(He follows DUNN
off L.)*

ROSALIE.   Ten minutes.   Ten minutes.   *(WILL.
crosses to door L. and closes door.)*

WILL.   *(L.C.)*   Why didn't you *tell* who did it?

ROSALIE.   *(C.)*   How could I?   Sure, I got no
idea in the world.   But I'm goin' to find out.   I'm
goin' to find out.

HELEN.   *(R.C.)*   But how, Mother, how?   *(HELEN
starts L.)*

ROSALIE.   Call them back.   Make them all come,
too.   I want them all.   *(HELEN runs off L.)*   Sir,
run down in the hall.   Do you know which is Mr.
Wales' overcoat?

WILL.   Yes, I think so.

ROSALIE.   See if you can find me a glove or something of his—and hurry.   *(WILL runs off L.   ROSA-
LIE stands in thought for a moment—puts chair C.
facing up stage.   WILL runs on again and hands her
a glove)*   Did you get it?

WILL.   *(L.C.)*   What are you going to do?

ROSALIE.   *(L.C.)*   Trick 'em.   Lie to 'em.   It's
for Nelly, do you blame me?

WILL.   What can I do to help?

ROSALIE.   Glory be!   It's a man after me own
heart.   I'm going to do something to put the fear of
God into the heart of that murderer.   Don't pay no
attention to me.   Watch them.   Don't look at me,
don't take your eyes off them.   I'm looking for one
of them to do something that will show us the way.
It's our only chance.

*(HELEN runs in at L.)*

HELEN.  They're coming.

ROSALIE.  Leave the door open so we can hear 'em.  (HELEN *does so and returns to her mother, standing* L. *of* ROSALIE)  Child, kiss me fer luck *(They kiss)*  It'll do no harm to kiss him, too. *(They kiss)*  Now son, can ye lie?

WILL  *Can I!*

ROSALIE.  (C.)  Here's the talk you're to make when they come in.  I'm goin' in a trance.  You'll tell 'em that I asked fer Mr. Wales' glove and the minute I got it in my hand, I went off like they see me.  Tell 'em ye thought maybe there might be some reason for it.  And then leave the rest to me.
*READY VOICE*

WILL.  I understand.

ROSALIE.  You stand here back of me.  I want them all in front of me.  (WILL *crosses back of* ROSALIE *to* R. *side of* ROSALIE'S *chair.*  HELEN *crosses* R. *of* ROSALIE *above her)*  Nelly, stand close by me.  Go further back.  *(Ready* VOICE.  HELEN *moves to* R. *of* ROSALIE)  That's right.  Now don't you move from there.  This'll be the realest trance ye ever saw, and the grandest fake.  When I come out, make 'em go away, tell 'em you're afraid it'll kill me to see anyone, just then.
*VOICES OFF LEFT*

*(She suddenly stiffens in her chair.  Lying rigid with her head thrown back on the headrest, and the hand in which she is holding* WALES' *glove stretched out straight in front of her.  Enter down* L., CROSBY, MISS EASTWOOD, STANDISH, TRENT, MRS. CROSBY, MRS. TRENT *and* MISS STANDISH.)*

CROSBY.  *(Crossing to up* L.C.*)*  What is it. Billy?

*(*MISS EASTWOOD L. *side of* ROSALIE'S *chair,* MRS.
TRENT *and* MRS. CROSBY L. *of settee* C.; TRENT
MISS ERSKINE *and* STANDISH *lower* L. *end of
settee.)*

STANDISH. What's happened?
WILL. *(*R. *side of* ROSALIE'S *chair)* I don't
know, exactly. We were talking about this awful
thing. She knew, of course, that her daughter
couldn't have done it, and she asked me to get her
something that had belonged to poor Wales. I got
a glove out of Wales' overcoat pocket and handed
it to her, and then all of a sudden she went stiff like
that. I don't know what it means.

*(The* OTHERS *draw closer to* ROSALIE. WILL *and*
HELEN *on the* R. *side of* ROSALIE'S *chair.* MISS
EASTWOOD *comes to* ROSALIE *and lays her hand
on her forehead.)*

MISS EASTWOOD. She's like ice, she's not——
*(Breaking up* C. *a few steps.)*
HELEN. Oh, no, it's a trance.

*(*MASON *enters* L. *down* L.*)*

MASON. I wouldn't touch her if I were you.
ROSALIE. *(Sitting in chair* R.C. *Speaking as
Laughing Eyes)* Hello, everybody. What you all
so solemn about, anyway? I've got a message
from a new friend. He don't want me to send it
—he wants to talk; ha, ha, ha, he thinks he can
talk, and he's only been here a little while. *(Still
speaking as Laughing Eyes)* He says you're all
fools. It's so plain, so plain. He's looking right
at the one who did it, right straight at the one who
did it. *(*WALES' *voice.)*
WALES' VOICE. I'm coming to you until you tell.

I can't speak names. You've got to tell. I'm coming, again and again and again, until you tell. Find the knife. You must find the knife. The marks will show. The marks will show.

*(MISS EASTWOOD shrieks and faints on L. end of settee. MASON is below end of settee looking at her. WILL is standing R. side and back of ROSALIE, looking eagerly about him. HELEN turns and looks at MISS EASTWOOD, MRS. CROSBY goes to MISS EASTWOOD on settee.)*

MASON.  This has got to stop.  *(Starts to ROSALIE's chair—L. side of it.)*

HELEN.  *(R. side of RORALEI's chair)*  You mustn't touch her.

MASON.  It's all right as far as the men are concerned, but look at that girl.  *(He points to MISS EASTWOOD on the settee)*  They'll all be fainting if this isn't stopped.  *(TRENT goes to ROSALIE.)*

WALES' VOICE.  Trent, let the medium alone. Do you understand?  Let the medium alone.

TRENT.  That's Wales' voice—and Wales is dead.

*(MASON crosses slowly to ROSALIE's chair. TRENT crosses L. above MASON to STANDISH—ROSALIE begins to mutter and moan. Suddenly she brings her hands together, and then throws her arms wide apart. WALES' glove sails out of her hand, and strikes MASON on the face. It falls to the floor. STANDISH exits very quietly door down L. MASON picks glove up—holding it in his hand—looks at it—suddenly drops it to the floor—turns to MRS. CROSBY.)*

MASON.  Mrs. Crosby, shall I take Miss Eastwood to your room for you?

Mrs. Crosby.  Yes, please, Phillip.

*(*Miss Erskine *crosses to door* L.  Mason *assists* Miss Eastwood *near seat and helps her from the room, exiting door down* L.  Mrs. Crosby *exits door* L.  Trent *wipes his hands with handkerchief.*  Rosalie *stirs uneasily and moans.*)*

Helen.  *(Standing* R. *side of* Rosalie's *chair)* Please leave her to me.  I'm afraid seeing you all here will trouble her.  I'm afraid she'll—— Oh, won't you please go?  *(The* Others *turn and go to door down* L.*—exit.*)

Crosby.  *(Below* L. *end of settee)*  Let me know if there's anything I can do.

Helen.  *(*Rosalie *moans again)*  Yes, yes. Only please go now.

*(*Crosby *exits door* L.  Will *runs quickly to the door at* L. *and closes it and turns to* Rosalie, *who is sitting up in her chair.)*

Rosalie.  *(Rises and crosses a step* R.*)*  Well?

Helen.  *(*R.C.*)*  It was the Eastwood girl.  Her face was terrible.  I was glad when she fainted.

Will.  *(*L.C.*)*  I think you're wrong.  Standish ran away.  He couldn't bear it.

Rosalie.  And that's all ye saw?  I told ye to use the brains that was back of yer eyes.

Will.  Well, of course, there was Trent.  You can't mean Trent?  Why, he's the kindest man in the world.  *(There is a pause)*  The letters.  If he's known the truth about the letters——  *(Breaks* L. *a step.)*

Helen.  *(Coming down to* L. *of* Rosalie's *chair and picking up glove)*  Mother, why did you throw that glove at Mason?

Rosalie.  Did it hit him?  Well, well, well.  Anyhow it was a good seance.

*(Will takes chair up l.  Rosalie crosses down r.c.)*

Helen.  *(l. side of Rosalie)*  Mother, you know —you've found out?

*(Will takes Rosalie's chair up to door r.c. and comes down to l. of Rosalie.)*

Rosalie.  Sure, it's wan thing to know and another to prove.

Helen.  *(l. of Rosalie)*  Mother, who was it?

Rosalie.  Child, child, do ye think it's a game we're playin'?  I got two or three minutes.  What I've got to do I've got to do quickly.

*READY KNOCK*

Helen.  But what, Mother, what?

Rosalie.  I don't know, I don't know.  Child, if you don't get away from me you'll drive me mad.

*READY KNOCK*

Will.  But can't we——

Rosalie.  This is no work for children. ' Leave me be and leave me think.  *(Will and Helen run off door l.—closing door)*  He'll never break in the world.  Never in all this world.  *(l.c.  Half in thought)*  Sure, Laughing Eyes, you're no good to me in the world.  We've faked all our lives, and now when I want the real thing I get nothing at all.  If I could find the knife, sure, there'd be marks av a hand on that.  But it's gone.  It's gone.  I can't let him get away with it.  I want a sign.  I want a sign.  Laughing Eyes, are we goin' to be beaten by a schemin', cold-hearted murderer?  *(Knock twice on table outside door down l., then count of five, rap twice more.  Ready lights.  Rosalie starts, looks hastily around the room)*  I didn't do that.

I didn't do that. *(She lifts her skirt and sees that her feet are still in her shoes.* It's come! After all the years, a real message. A real message. I'll take it in the dark, believin' and trustin' that I'm to be shown. *(Lights out. Crosses down to door L.—pushes light switch. All lights in room out. The spot from the window shines on the ceiling, is brilliantly illuminating the knife.* ROSALIE *crosses to chair* C.) Laughing Eyes, have you a message for me? *(She looks up at knife in ceiling)* Look at it! Glory be to God. The knife!

*(The door at* L. *opens.* POLLOCK *stands in the doorway. He sees that the lights are out and turns them on. Then he sees* ROSALIE, *who is standing* C., *facing front as in a trance.)*
*LIGHTS ON*

POLLOCK. Excuse me, Madam. I knocked twice, but you didn't hear me.

ROSALIE. I heard ye. It was a message just the same.

POLLOCK. The Inspector says have you got anything you want to tell him? *(*ROSALIE *stands lost in thought.* POLLOCK *looks at her for a moment and then nervously begins to set the chair below table up* R. *corner of set. He notices that the window blind is up, goes over and pulls it down and draws the curtains. He then comes back to* ROSALIE *above table* R.)* The Inspector says have you got anything you want to tell him?

*(*ROSALIE *crosses down* R. *in front of table.* DONO-HUE *enters from* L.)*

DONOHUE. *(Crosses to* C.)* Time's about up. *(He laughs)* Well?

ROSALIE. *(Below table* R.)* I want them all here. All of them. Every one.

DONOHUE.   What for?

ROSALIE.   You're going to hear the murderer confess.

DONOHUE.   Pollock, ask Mr. Crosby to bring everyone here.   *(Crosses R. to above table.)*

POLLOCK.   Very good, sir.   *(He exits L. DONOHUE takes out his watch and stands with it in his hand, watching ROSALIE.   She stands lost in her dreams.   DUNN enters with HELEN O'NEILL down L.)*

DUNN.   Here she is, Inspector.

DONOHUE.   Come here, Miss.   *(HELEN crosses to DONOHUE.   To DUNN)*   Go get a taxi.

*(DUNN turns and exits L.   The OTHERS enter and stand crowding in the doorway.   WILL pushes through and crosses and stands by HELEN up R.C. right end of settee.)*

CROSBY.   *(Up L.C.)*   What is it?   You sent for us.

DONOHUE.   *(Between table and settee C.)*   She says her daughter's not guilty.   I gave her ten minutes to find out who is.   The time's up.   *(He puts his watch back in his pocket.   He turns to ROSALIE)*   Well?

*(ROSALIE stands rigid.   There is a long pause.)*

ROSALIE.   *(Below table R.)*   You that's hidin', come out.

*READY DOOR*

DONOHUE.   Come on.   *(He takes HELEN by the hand.   They go up R. above table.)*

ROSALIE.   *(Lower end of table R.)*   You that's skulkin', come out!   The message has come.   I call on the spirit of Edward Wales.   I call on the spirit

of Edward Wales.   Now you that's killed two men,
look!

*(The door at* L. *of fireplace slowly swings open.*
   MASON, *with a cry of horror, pushes through
   the crowd at the doorway, which parts to let
   him through.   He follows the spirit he sees mov-
   ing across the stage until he is at* C. *and a little
   above the table.*   MRS. TRENT, ERSKINE *and*
   STANDISH *below door down* L.   TRENT, MRS.
   CROSBY, MISS EASTWOOD C. *above door* L.   *All
   watch* MASON.   *Suddenly the window curtains
   are thrown back, the shade runs up noisily and
   the lights go down.   The street light strikes the
   knife in the ceiling, as it begins to fall.*   MA-
   SON'S *eye follows the light.   He sees the knife
   and gives a cry of horror as it strikes the table
   and sticks in front of him.*   MASON *rushes up
   stage end of table* R.)

   MASON.   *(With a cry)*   I can't fight the dead.
I can't fight the dead!

*(Slowly* ROSALIE *points at him.   The* OTHERS *stand
            and stare.)*

   ROSALIE.   Go on, tell it.   *(Lower* R. *side of
table* R.)
   MASON.   I had to do it.   I was afraid Mr. Wales
would know.
   ROSALIE.   You killed them both?
   MASON.   Yes.
   ROSALIE.   Mr. Wales to prevent his finding out
about Spencer Lee?
   MASON.   Yes.
   ROSALIE.   And Spencer Lee?

         *(*WILL *up* R.C. *above settee* C.)

MASON. He ought to have been killed. I'd been waiting for years to kill him.

ROSALIE. Why?

MASON. That's between him and me. He smashed my life, and by God, I got him. He knows why I killed him, I told him I would. I'm glad I did. I only wish I could have done it over and over again. That's all.

ROSALIE. Why did you kill Spencer Lee?

MASON. He took her away from me. She was the one thing in the world and he took her away from me. I went to Paris to forget and all I could do was to remember. Then she died, and I made up my mind that he must die, too.

DONOHUE. How did you get the knife in the ceiling?

MASON. I threw it. Just as I threw a knife into Spencer Lee's back. I stood in the doorway of his room and told him I'd come to kill him, and he ran for his revolver, and as he ran I threw the knife into his back. Then I picked up my knife, and walked away. No one saw me. I was quite safe. Quite safe until she came. And unseen hands pushed me forward. Unseen hands have pointed the way. She's not human. Lee's message came through her—you all heard Wales speak; out of her lips we heard Wales' voice. He said he'd come back, again and again and again. And then he came! I saw him as he came through the door! God Almighty, you can't fight the dead! *(He turns suddenly and walks to door L. As he opens it SER-GEANT DUNN steps into the room.)*

DONOHUE. That's your man, Sergeant.

DUNN. *(Putting his hand on MASON's arm)* You got him?

DONOHUE. Yes, I got him.

DUNN. Great work, chief, great work. *(He takes MASON off down L.)*    WARN

*(HELEN crosses down to lower end of table R.)*

ROSALIE. *(As they disappear from view)* The poor young fella, the poor young fella.

DONOHUE. Ladies and gentlemen, you are all quite at liberty. *(He goes toward door L.)*

CROSBY. Thank you, Inspector, for your consideration.

DONOHUE. Not at all, it was the best way out of it.

ROSALIE. Inspector. *(Coming below table R. to R.C.)*

DONOHUE. *(Half turning)* Yes?

ROSALIE. My congratulations.

*(He looks at her for a moment, then turns back and shakes hands with her.)*

DONOHUE. You were quite right about me. I was a damn fool. *(He exits at L.)*

*(HELEN coming below table R.)*

MRS. TRENT. *(Turning to her father up L.C. with a cry)* Oh, Daddy, Daddy! I lied about her. I lied about her.

*(CROSBY takes her in his arms, up L. HELEN crosses to ROSALIE from below table R.)*

ROSALIE. *(C.)* There's nothing but happiness comin' to ye. The spirits tell me ye're the favorite child af fortune. You'll have wealth and prosperity and happiness. You'll marry the man ye love, and ye'll be happy——

## CURTAIN

# ELECTRICIAN'S PLOT

## ACT I

Foots full rose, ambers ¾ at rise. Light switch down stage side of door down left. Hanging lamps, post lamps, table lamps, lit. Amber strip in doorway down left, lit. One light strip amber, in doorway R.C. and L.C. Two light strip amber, hung on fireplace backing. Two blue bunches outside window right, lit. Baby amber shooting across stage from window right. Baby amber striking mantel up center from window right. Amber baby down left at proscenium arch shooting across stage, lit. Blue baby focused to strike Rosalie in chair center from window right, OUT AT RISE. White frost spot in position outside of window right to strike ceiling on cue OUT AT RISE.

### 1st Cue

When Rosalie lifts table first time, sneak off baby down stage left, also baby from window right that starts across stage.

### 2nd Cue

After Pollock locks door down left, all entrance strips and baby down left, out.

### 3rd Cue

When Crosby pushes button, all foots out. Brackets out, lamp posts out.  Amber babies at window right, out.  At same time, white spotlight on ceiling, LIT.

### 4th Cue

When Will pulls chain on table lamp right end of settee, table lamp out.  Two babies from window out.

### 5th Cue

When Crosby says "The reflection on the ceiling is too strong," Will pulls chain on table lamp right end of settee table lamp and two babies from window right, LIT.

### 6th Cue

Will pulls down window shade, spot on ceiling and blue bunches OUT.  Then when Will pulls chain on the table lamp right end of settee, table lamp, two babies outside window right, OUT.

### 7th Cue

When Crosby says "Lights, son," table lamp right end of settee, LIT.  Two babies from window LIT. Amber foots ¼ LIT.  Bring on blue baby outside window right.

### 8th Cue

When Will pulls chain on table lamp right end of settee, table lamp, two babies, amber foots, OUT, leaving blue spot, LIT.

### 9th Cue

When Crosby says "Lights, son," table lamp right end of settee, LIT; two amber babies, LIT; amber foots, ⅜ LIT.

NOTE: All house lights in front (Auditorium) must be OUT when Rosalie and ladies enter after Rosalie has been searched. This is very important.

## ACT II

Amber foots, half up. Hanging brackets, lamp posts, table lamps, entrance strips, LIT. Amber baby down in left first entrance, LIT. Blue bunches outside of window right, LIT. Fireplace, LIT. Lights stand during this act.

## ACT III

Everything OUT at RISE except amber strip and amber baby in left first entrance and blue bunches outside of window, right, which are LIT.

### 1st Cue

After prayer, Rosalie raises windowshade, white spot or knife in ceiling, LIT.

### 2nd Cue

Inspector pushes lights lit, amber foots ½, table lamps, brackets, post lights, LIT.

NOTE: No lights in entrance R C., L.C. and fireplace.

### 3rd Cue

Rosalie pushes light switch, foots, table lamps, brackets, post lights OUT.  Spot on knife from outside window right, LIT.

### 4th Cue

Pollock pushes light switch, amber foots, table lamps, brackets, post lights, LIT same as AT RISE. Spot on knife, OUT.

### 5th Cue

Rosalie says "I call on the spirit of Edward Wales," start to dim foots to $\frac{1}{8}$.  Must be down on word "look."  As window shade flies up, spot or knife, LIT.  As knife leaves ceiling spot OUT and amber foots, flash up, full.

## SCENE PLOT FOR ACT I

Italian Room in Roscoe Crosby's home, New York. A handsomely furnished square room. 1. Door opening on stage down L. 2. Door opening on stage at back L.C. 3. Door opening on stage R.C. 4. Large fireplace C. at back. The fireplace with antique fire-dogs must be large enough for man to make an entrance coming through chimney. 5. Large window over R. in arch. 6. Platform one step high running full length of window, which is three sashes long. Trick blind on centre pane. Curtains on pole on centre windows to work on cue. 7. Up C. in front of fireplace facing up stage, large chesterfield sofa two feet wide. 8. Facing audience another large chesterfield sofa, C., sofas back to back. 9. At each end of sofas small console tables. Console table at right end of sofa is the trick table which Rosalie lifts. On console tables at either end of sofa, table lamps. On console table left end of sofa, fancy cigarette box with cigarettes and match-box and ash-tray. 10. Right of the door, R.C., large antique Italian chest. 11. Left of door, L.C., large antique chest. Vases on chests. On flat over L. large tapestry. 12. Against wall over L. running up and down stage long ornate Italian chest. 13. At either end of this chest Italian lamps, seven feet high, standing on floor. Below door down L., on flat, an antique clock. 14. Below door down L., arm-chair. 15. Left side of fireplace chair with cushion seat. On mantel two large antique vases. 16. Right side of fireplace, chair with cushion seat. 17. Large arm-chair. 18. Over right is a large library table sitting diagonally up and down stage. On table: book-rack with four books, desk-pad, stationery-holder with stationery, pens, pencils, ink-box, magazines. 19. Arm-chair back of table. 20. Chair below table. 21. Chair above table. 22. On platform in window arch, long seat. 23. Below window arch long arm-chair. 24. Large wall lanterns, on up stage and down stage, end of window arch. Plush valence or drapery for windows. Rugs on ground cloth. On flat right of doors up R.C. small-sized, painted image of the Virgin. Interior backing for door down L., up L.C., and R.C. Fireplace backing. Exterior backing for window over R. 25. Off stage down L. large Italian table with two bronze vases, and a shrine of the Virgin on it. Off stage R.C. are eight small chairs, to be brought on stage on cue during First Act. In ceiling, directly over table R., is a double slot to hold knives. During First Act, after William puts out table lamp, *after* Miss Eastwood's *scream*, the knife in down stage slot is let down in sight of audience. *Seen with point sticking in ceiling*. Between Second and Third Acts, the knife that falls on cue, during Third Act, is placed up stage slot in ceiling, with point downwards. Setting the knife down in view of audience in First Act, as well as releasing the second knife so that it falls, and sticks in table during Third Act, is worked by strings off stage R.

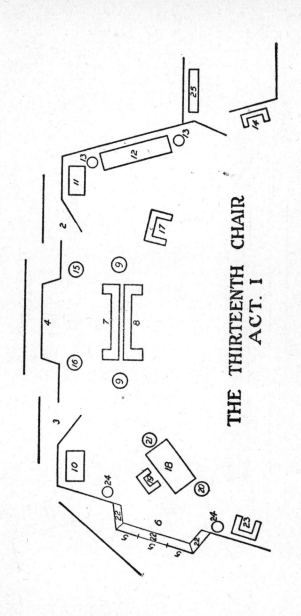

THE THIRTEENTH CHAIR
ACT. I

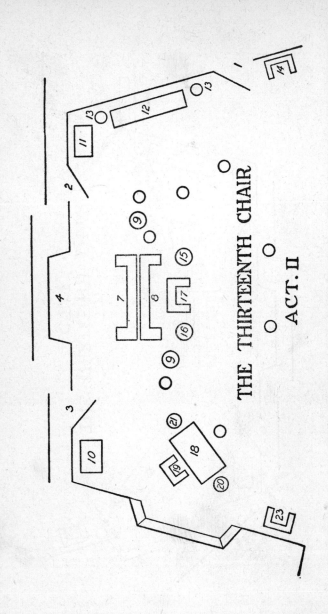

THE THIRTEENTH CHAIR

ACT. II